THE
CROSS-STITCH
COLLECTION

This edition published in 1995 by
Shooting Star Press Inc.,
230 Fifth Avenue
Suite 1212
New York
NY 10001

Produced by Marshall Cavendish Books, London
(a division of Marshall Cavendish Partworks Ltd)

Copyright © Marshall Cavendish 1995
Foreword copyright © Melinda Coss 1995

ISBN 1 57335 132 6

Library of Congress Cataloging in Publication Data:
A catalog record for this book is available from
the Library of Congress

Printed and bound in Italy

Jacket border panel stitched by Linda Kippax,
Madeira Threads (UK) Ltd

Some of this material has previously appeared in
the Marshall Cavendish partwork *Discovering Needlecraft*

Contents

Foreword

Melinda Coss

*I*n our highly technological age, an "embroidery epidemic" has to be considered a phenomenon. Yet here we are, nearly at the year 2000, and everywhere you look people are sitting with needles and threads, as cozy now, under electric light bulbs, as they were a hundred years ago, stitching by the glow of an oil lamp.

"What's the fascination?" ask the uninitiated. But how do you explain the pleasure of transforming richly colored, silky smooth threads into finely patterned and textured fabrics? Stitching, as any embroiderer will tell you, is obsessive, and cross-stitching in particular, with its simple, repetitive technique, provides a comforting and therapeutic way to end a stressful day. Add to that the portability of a needlework project, the low cost of the materials, and the satisfaction of producing your own personal heirloom, and it is perhaps not so surprising that needlecraft remains one of our most popular leisure activities.

Through my years as a needlecraft designer, I have established that most stitchers share two major problems. The first is that they always underestimate their own abilities, and the second is that they never have enough designs to choose from. This book should provide the solutions.

Packed with bright ideas and delicious projects, the book has something that will appeal to all tastes and levels of skill. It talks you through the stitching process from beginning to end, and what is not explained in words is there for all to see on the clearly graphed charts and beautiful photographs. It also has a collection of hints and tips that will help you make sure that your stitched designs have a highly professional finish. In addition, it explains in detail how to turn your needlework into a decorative and useful item.

Many stitchers dread the finishing process; but often we only have to succeed at something once to realize that we are cleverer than we think, and this confidence can lead on to all manner of new and satisfying accomplishments. The secret is to read the instructions carefully and to begin with a relatively simple project, such as a greeting card. Take it step by step, and before you know it you will find yourself making cushions and framing pictures like a true expert.

Needlecraft is not simply about following patterns and using specific materials. It is also a valuable means of self-expression. You can stitch with wool, ribbons, silk, and even strips of fabric, and you don't have to use special embroidery materials to achieve pleasing results. Try using the motifs and techniques in this book to create your own individual statement. The tile sachet motif, for example, could be repeated in numerous colorways to create a panel for a pillow, or the kite motif could be cross-stitched in wool yarn on a child's plain sweater. Work some beads into your cross-stitch and make bands and borders into curtain ties or shelf trims. Once you gain confidence, you will realize that your only limitation is your imagination.

On a final note, if you have children around the house, do share your skills with them. I, for one, hope to live long enough to see my grandchildren stitching, although I suspect they may be doing it on electro-magnetic fibers with automatic laser-powered needle-pushers. In the meantime, enjoy yourselves and this book, which will undoubtedly provide you with many hours of inspiration.

Melinda Coss.

The Projects

Introduction

*C*ross-stitch is one of the most enduringly popular of the multitude of embroidery techniques. Because it is straightforward to work, it is simple for the beginner, but its lasting appeal has much to do with the fact that it is extremely versatile, and its beauty is undeniable.

The projects that have been collected together here provide a wide variety of items to stitch, and they are designed to appeal to beginners and cross-stitch addicts alike. The clear charts are easy to follow, and the finished pieces can be enjoyed for years to come by you, a member of your family, or a lucky friend. Cross-stitched items are popular presents, and those in this book range from greeting cards that can be completed in an evening to a selection of beautiful, more intricate floral pillows and a delightful bell-pull featuring some of the best-loved and most common birds of Britain, each one perched in a different kind of tree.

Some of the projects, such as the mirror case or napkin rings, would make excellent items to sell at charity bazaars – they can be made quickly enough that, with a little planning, you could stitch several in a variety of colors to appeal to different tastes. Perhaps one of the more complicated pieces – the breakfast linen set or one of the beautiful pictures – could be donated and sold at an auction or used as a prize in a money-spinning raffle.

There is also a selection of presents suitable for a new baby or a special child. The baby's wall hanging is in fact a commemorative sampler that could be completed (by unsuperstitious stitchers, of course) except for the baby's name and birth date, ready to be finished in a flash and presented to proud new parents to welcome a new arrival.

The more complicated projects have in them various elements that can be extracted and used individually to make small items such as greeting cards or miniature pictures. Some of the designs lend themselves to being stitched separately and then grouped – the birds on the bell-pull or the ducks on the baby's crib cover, for example – could be mounted individually and hung as pictures next to each other. If you are new to cross-stitch, you may want to read pages 105–6 before you begin. Then choose your project, study the chart, pick up your needle, and start to stitch. But be warned: cross-stitch can be addictive!

A NOTE ABOUT THREADS
The stranded floss or other threads specified in each project have been used to work the items shown in the photographs. If you are unable to purchase the materials exactly as specified, it will still be possible to work the project, but the look may be somewhat altered. Most brands of threads have similar or equivalent colors from which to choose, but the color match may not be exact.

Tea rose pillow

Two full-blown roses evoke images of summer flower beds.
You can almost smell their heady perfume.

Tea rose pillow

YOU WILL NEED

- **20 × 21in 14-count navy blue aida fabric**
- **Paterna Persian yarn, one skein each of:**

    Pale coral 865   864 Coral

    Sugar pink 915   912 Mauve-pink

    Dark terracotta D211   900 Crimson

    Bright green 692   663 Blue-green

    Dull green 602   D516 Dark green

    Bottle green 660

- **Two skeins each of:**

    Medium pink 932   D234 Red-pink

    Olive green 650

- **Tapestry needle**
- **17 × 18in backing fabric**
- **16in square pillow form**
- **2yd thick pink twisted cord**

Tea roses in glorious shades of pink and coral are shown in full bloom on the front of this pillow. They are worked in cross-stitch on a dark blue aida fabric, using Paterna Persian yarn rather than the more usual stranded floss. The motifs are typical of Victorian-era Berlin woolwork designs, which often featured roses of this sort, although they would have been worked on canvas rather than aida.

This pillow would look beautiful in any living room, whether you have plain, modern furnishings or a more chintzy, traditional décor. It is also perfect for a sunroom, placed on a basketwork armchair or an ornate metal-work bench. The finished pillow measures $15\frac{1}{2} \times 16$in and is trimmed with a harmonizing pink twisted cord.

BEFORE YOU BEGIN

Overcast or bind the edges of the aida fabric to prevent them from fraying. Mark the center of the fabric horizontally and vertically with running stitches in a light-colored thread. Mark the center of the color chart shown opposite in the same way with pencil lines. This will make it easier for you to position the stitches correctly when you begin to work from the chart.

Mount the fabric in a scroll frame or a large embroidery hoop to keep it taut during stitching. It will then be easier to maintain an even tension when you are working the cross-stitches, giving the finished embroidery a more professional look. If you use a hoop, you will need to move it around as you complete each area of stitching. So that you do not spoil the stitching you have already done, place a layer of acid-free tissue paper over it before fixing the top ring of the hoop. Remember to remove the hoop at the end of each stitching session, as it can mark the fabric permanently if it is left on for too long.

STITCHING THE ROSES

Follow the color chart on the opposite page to work the design. Each colored square equals one cross-stitch worked over four blocks of the aida fabric (two up and two across), using just one strand of the Paterna Persian yarn in the needle. As there are so many different shades of pink and green in the roses, you may find it helpful to thread your yarn on to

KEY

Paterna Persian yarn, as used in the Tea rose pillow:

	Pale coral – 865 (A)
	Coral – 864 (B)
	Sugar pink – 915 (C)
	Mauve-pink – 912 (D)
	Dark terracotta – D211 (E)
	Crimson – 900 (F)
	Bright green – 692 (G)
	Blue-green – 663 (H)
	Dull green – 602 (I)
	Dark green – D516 (J)
	Bottle green – 660 (K)
	Olive green – 650 (L)
	Medium pink – 932 (M)
	Red-pink – D234 (N)

STITCH DETAILS

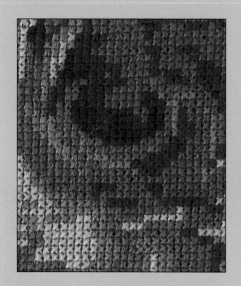

The upper rose is worked using the darker shades of pink and crimson. Sugar pink is used to add shading to some of the lower petals.

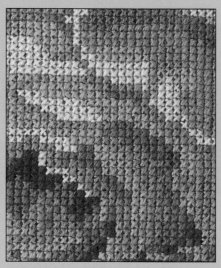

For the lower rose, lighter shades of pink are combined with two shades of coral to create a more subtle effect.

Work the leaves using all shades of green. Dark green, bottle green, and olive green form the centers while blue-green is used for shading.

project cards. You can buy these in notions departments or needlecraft stores, or you can make them yourself by punching holes along the edge of a strip of stiff cardboard. Cut the yarn into lengths of not more than 18in and loop them through the holes, writing the number and name of the shade beside each one. It will then be easier to find the correct color as you come to it on the chart. When you have completed the design, keep the project card as a record of your work along with at least one skein band to remind you of any care instructions.

Begin stitching at the center of the chart, working the lower petals of the top right-hand rose and moving gradually upward. To secure your yarn, leave a short end at the back and work your first few stitches over it; to finish off neatly, pass the needle under the last few stitches at the back and then cut off the end of the yarn so that it does not get caught in subsequent stitching. When you are working the design, complete one area of color at a time before moving on to the next. With all the small patches of color in the rose petals and leaves, you can speed up your work by threading several needles with the different colors and using the appropriate needle as you require it. Keep the needles that are not in use pinned in the margin of the fabric, well away from the stitching area.

To add depth and definition to the roses, each one has been worked in several shades of pink and red. The top rose is worked in six different shades, ranging from very dark to very light: crimson (900), dark terracotta (D211), red-pink (D234), medium pink (932), mauve-pink (912), and sugar pink (915). When you have completed this rose, work the leaves around it in various shades of green. Then stitch the lower rose. This flower shares some of the same colors with the upper rose (dark terracotta, red-pink, mauve-pink, and medium pink), but brings in coral (864) and pale coral (865) so that it is much softer and looks subtly different from the other rose.

FINISHING THE PILLOW

When you have finished embroidering the rose design, remove the fabric from the hoop or frame and check that you have not missed any stitches as these will be difficult to add once the pillow has been assembled. Press the stitching from the back over a lightly padded surface. Trim the aida so that it measures 17in wide and 18in high, taking care to cut along the rows of holes in the aida fabric to make sure that you get a straight line.

Cut the backing fabric to match. Place it with the aida, right sides facing, and stitch around three sides with backstitch, taking a 1/2in seam allowance and leaving the lower edge open for

turning right side out. Clip across the upper corners to remove the excess fabric, turn the cover to the right side, and insert the pillow form. Sew up the fourth side with slipstitches, leaving a small gap in the center of the seam. Attach the twisted cord with slipstitches, finishing the raw ends by inserting them in the gap left in the seam.

HANDY

For cross-stitch to look smooth and professionally stitched, it is important to work all the crosses with the top part slanting in the same direction. This is especially true with the large crosses worked in wool yarn on this pillow, as the larger and chunkier the stitches, the more obvious it will be if one is worked in the wrong direction.

As the rose motifs have no obvious right way up, you will find it helpful to mark the top of the fabric with a large cross made in the same direction as the ones you are working in the design. This will tell you at a glance which way up your embroidery should be and which way to stitch the crosses, and is particularly useful when you get your embroidery out again after a long break.

HINTS

Cactus pillow

The superb display of pink cactus flowers on this cross-stitch pillow
will make an impact in any room.

Cactus pillow

A floral display always looks beautiful in cross-stitch, and this one is no exception. The flowers here are rather unusual, as they belong to a plant called the rat's-tail cactus (*Aporocactus Flagelliformis* is its Latin name). In ideal conditions, the flower-bearing stems on this plant can grow to over two yards long and are very suitable for brightening up your hanging baskets.

The cactus is displayed in a blue-and-white china pot, the design of which is echoed in the wide chevron border. The simplicity of the border is very pleasing as a contrast to the rest of the design. With another border of un-worked fabric around this, the finished pillow measures 12 inches square. Some of the flowers are positioned outside the frame, which gives the cactus a three-dimensional effect, as though the stems are growing out toward you.

Closely matching shades of pink are used for the flowers to make them realistic and subtle. Their centers are highlighted by yellow stamens. The leaves are equally life-like, punctuated along their length by small, pale brown spines.

FOLLOWING THE CHART

The chart for the cactus design is shown on the opposite page. Each colored square equals one cross-stitch worked over one square of aida fabric. The colors of Madeira 6-stranded embroidery floss to use are given in the key.

Where squares on the chart are shown divided diagonally, with half in one color and half in another, work three-quarter and quarter cross-stitches (see page 54 for details of how to form these stitches). The effect of using these part cross-stitches is to give a smooth outline, adding to the realistic look of the plant and the pot.

To make it easier for you to place the stitches correctly when you are working the embroidery, mark the horizontal and vertical center lines of the fabric with running stitches in a contrasting colored sewing thread. These will be removed when the embroidery is complete. Mark the center lines of the chart in pencil to correspond.

STITCHING THE CACTUS

Overcast or bind the edges of the aida fabric to prevent them from fraying while you are stitching. Stretch the fabric in an embroidery hoop or frame if you wish, as this will help to give a smoother, more regular finish to your embroidery stitches. Work with two strands of embroidery floss in the needle throughout, using lengths of no more than 18in to prevent the thread from tangling and wearing thin.

Begin stitching at the center of the design, following the chart carefully so that you count the stitches correctly. To secure your thread at the beginning, leave a short end at the back and work the first few cross-stitches over it. To finish off neatly, pass your needle through the last few stitches worked at the back and cut the thread off short. In this way, it will not become tangled in subsequent stitching and

produce an unsightly effect on the right side of the work.

Work the design in blocks of color, finishing off one area of color before beginning the next. Do not pass long strands of thread across the back of the fabric from one part of the design to another of the same color as they may show through at the front of the work, or get caught up in other stitching and cause lumps and bumps.

YOU WILL NEED

- **16 × 16in 14-count white aida fabric**

- **Madeira 6-stranded embroidery floss, one skein each of:**

Crimson 0509	0507 Cerise
Bright pink 0610	0609 Light pink
Pale yellow 0101	0112 Yellow
Flesh 2308	2011 Honey
Sugar pink 0503	1414 Pale green
Bright green 1609	1608 Sage green
Dark green 1314	1808 Dk pinkish gray
Lt pinkish gray 1806	1804 Silver gray
Medium blue 0911	0913 Dark blue

- **Tapestry needle**
- **14 × 14in backing fabric**
- **12in square pillow form**
- **1½ yd blue twisted cord**

KEY

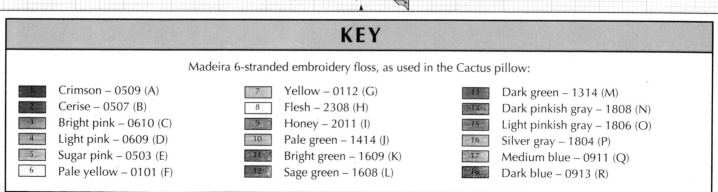

Madeira 6-stranded embroidery floss, as used in the Cactus pillow:

1 Crimson – 0509 (A)	7 Yellow – 0112 (G)	13 Dark green – 1314 (M)
2 Cerise – 0507 (B)	8 Flesh – 2308 (H)	14 Dark pinkish gray – 1808 (N)
3 Bright pink – 0610 (C)	9 Honey – 2011 (I)	15 Light pinkish gray – 1806 (O)
4 Light pink – 0609 (D)	10 Pale green – 1414 (J)	16 Silver gray – 1804 (P)
5 Sugar pink – 0503 (E)	11 Bright green – 1609 (K)	17 Medium blue – 0911 (Q)
6 Pale yellow – 0101 (F)	12 Sage green – 1608 (L)	18 Dark blue – 0913 (R)

Begin stitching the cactus leaf at the center of the design in bright green (1609) and sage green (1608) with the spine markings in honey (2011). Then work the flower to the left in shades of pink. Leave all the yellow centers of the flowers until the rest of the cross-stitching is complete, as these are worked in French knots. Continue working the top part of the design, moving gradually from one flower to the next by stitching the leaves in between them. Around the flowerpot, there is some deep shading in dark green (1314). As you work out toward the tips of the leaves, they change in color to pale green (1414).

Now continue with the stitching in the lower part of the design, finishing off the leaves and flowers here. Work the pattern on the flowerpot on the left in medium blue (0911) and dark blue (0913) with a horizontal band near the top in dark pinkish gray (1808). The shading is worked in light pinkish gray (1806) and silver gray (1804).

Finally, stitch the chevron border in medium blue. Count the squares on the chart very carefully, as the border will not meet at the corners correctly if you miscount. When the stitching is complete, add the French knots (see page 109) that form the flower centers. Use pale yellow (0101) and yellow (0112).

FINISHING THE PILLOW

Press the work carefully from the wrong side over a lightly padded surface so as not to flatten the raised stitches. Also check at this stage that you have not missed any stitches as they will be difficult to add once the pillow is finished. Trim the aida fabric to measure 13½in square, making sure that you leave an equal amount of unworked fabric on each side of the chevron border. Cut the backing fabric to the same size.

With right sides facing, pin the front and the back of the pillow together and then backstitch around three sides so that you leave an unstitched area 15 aida squares wide all around the edge of the design. Leave the bottom edge open for turning right side out. Turn the cover right side out, insert the pillow form, and sew up the fourth side with slip-stitches, leaving a small opening in the center of the seam. Slipstitch the twisted cord around the outer edges to cover the seam. Insert the ends of the cord into the opening in the bottom edge to finish them and then slipstitch this to close it.

STITCH DETAILS

The cactus flowers are worked in various shades of pink, which are blended to create a very realistic effect. Texture is created by adding yellow French knots in the centers.

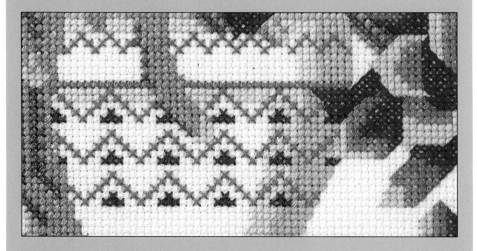

The pattern on the ceramic flowerpot is worked in two shades of blue with a stripe in dark pinkish gray. The shading is worked in light pinkish gray and silver gray.

Medium blue is used to work the wide chevron border around the cactus plant. Where the chevrons meet at the corners, an interesting diamond pattern is created.

Clematis pillow

*This finely shaded cross-stitch design of clematis flowers has
the delicate look of a watercolor painting.*

Clematis pillow

Delicate pink and white flowers outlined with a blue-gray backstitch form a striking pattern on this botanical pillow.

A popular variety of clematis – "Nelly Moser" – is depicted on the front of this beautiful pillow. It is worked in cross-stitch with backstitch outlines on cream aida fabric, and has been given areas of texture at the flower centers with groups of French knots. The impressive striped petals look almost as if they have been painted in watercolor and show the delicate shading that can be achieved with carefully placed colors of stranded floss which are very close in tone.

The border of clematis leaves echoes the central motif and is an important part of the design. Although the pattern is actually repeated around all four sides, it gives the impression of a random arrangement of leaves cleverly placed to fill the space between the inner and outer bands. These bands are worked in a simple geometrical pattern in colors which complement the main design. The finishing touch is the Latin name for this plant – *Ranunculaceae* – which is stitched at the lower left-hand corner in the manner in which a botanical print might be labeled.

BEFORE YOU BEGIN

Overcast or bind the edges of the aida fabric to prevent it from fraying as you work. Mark the center lines horizontally and vertically with lines of basting to help you when you are counting the stitches from the chart. If you wish, stretch the fabric in a scroll frame to keep it taut while you are stitching the design; this will help to give an even tension and a professional-looking result.

The design is shown on the chart opposite. Each colored square equals one cross-stitch.

The heavier lines around the petals and leaves on the main motif indicate backstitching. The colors of stranded floss to use are shown in the key. You may find it useful to cut your stranded floss into working lengths of 18 inches in advance and loop them through holes in a project card. Write down the shade number and name beside each one, and you will then find it easier to locate the appropriate color as you come to it on the chart. Project cards are available from good needlecraft and department stores, or, if you wish,

The border pattern is shown only on the lower edge of the chart. To work the remaining three sides, repeat this border within the marked lines.

Ranunculaceae

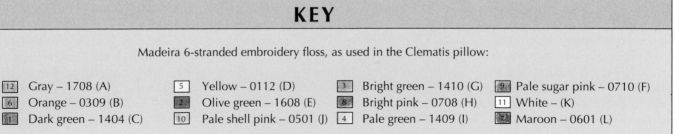

KEY

Madeira 6-stranded embroidery floss, as used in the Clematis pillow:

12	Gray – 1708 (A)	5	Yellow – 0112 (D)	3	Bright green – 1410 (G)	9	Pale sugar pink – 0710 (F)
6	Orange – 0309 (B)	2	Olive green – 1608 (E)	8	Bright pink – 0708 (H)	11	White – (K)
1	Dark green – 1404 (C)	10	Pale shell pink – 0501 (J)	4	Pale green – 1409 (I)	7	Maroon – 0601 (L)

bright idea

If you wish to fill the center panel of this pillow completely with clematis flowers, you can work the bottom right-hand corner flower motif in the two empty corners. By adding some leaves and stems to create a diagonal effect, the added flowers will blend in well with the existing motif. For the lower left-hand corner, use the motif exactly as it appears on the chart and place it 10 aida squares in from each edge. For the top right-hand corner, work the motif upside down, placing it 10 aida squares from the top edge and 5 aida squares from the side.

For the top right-hand corner, turn the motif upside down.

For the bottom left-hand motif (not shown), simply repeat the motif, placing it 10 aida squares from the edge of the border.

Repeat this motif in the top right and bottom left-hand corners.

54) to give a smooth slanting line. These are shown on the chart by squares with diagonal lines crossing them and with each part colored in a different shade of green.

Next work the clematis flowers with their shaded petals. Use the three shades of pink – pale shell pink (0501), pale sugar pink (0710), and bright pink (0708) – with white and a few areas of gray (1708). The flower centers are a combination of yellow cross-stitches and French knots (see page 109) worked alternately in orange (0309) and maroon (0601).

ADDING THE BORDER

Begin by stitching the inner band of the border in dark green (1404) and pale sugar pink. Count carefully from the top flowers to make sure that you begin on the right row of aida squares, as the border will not join up correctly otherwise. When the inner band is complete, work the leaf design around the edge in pale green, dark green, bright green, and olive green with tiny blossoms in pale shell pink with yellow centers. Work the outer band around the leaf border in dark green and bright pink. The geometric design is the same as the inner band, but the small chevrons point in the opposite direction.

WORKING THE BACKSTITCHES

To give a delicate outline to parts of the design, the petals and leaves on the main motif are outlined in backstitching. Use one strand of embroidery floss for this. Outline the petals in gray and the leaves and main stems in olive green. The narrow stems in the design are worked in backstitch in bright green, using two strands of floss. Finally stitch the Latin name for the clematis plant with one strand of dark green floss.

FINISHING THE PILLOW

When you have finished embroidering the design, check carefully that you have not missed any stitches. If necessary, press the work from the wrong side over a padded surface so that you do not flatten the stitches. Trim the aida fabric to 1/2in all around. Place the embroidery on the backing fabric, right sides together. Stitch them together with backstitch, working into the row of holes alongside the border. Leave an opening on the fourth side to insert the pillow form. Clip the corners and turn right side out. Insert the pillow form and sew up the opening with small, neat slipstitches.

you can make your own by punching a row of holes down one edge of a rectangular strip of cardboard.

WORKING THE FLOWERS

Find the center point of the chart and begin stitching here. Complete all the areas of cross-stitch before working any backstitching. Use two strands of embroidery floss for all the cross-stitching. Work the central bud in pale green (1409) and bright green (1410), with a small amount of pale sugar pink (0710) at the tip. To secure your thread end at the beginning, work the first few stitches over it; to finish off neatly when you complete an area of color, slip the needle under the last few stitches at the back.

Continue the embroidery by extending the stem out at each end of the bud, then complete the other leaves and buds in pale green, bright green, and olive green (1608). Finish off one area of color before beginning the next and make sure you do not carry long strands across the back of the work, as these may show through on the right side or get caught in subsequent stitching. Some parts of the leaves and buds are worked with three-quarter and quarter cross-stitches (see page

Gladioli pillow

A glorious design of delicately worked gladioli flowers makes this pillow
a beautiful accessory for a sunroom or living room sofa.

Gladioli pillow

YOU WILL NEED

- **20 × 21in 14-count cream aida fabric**

- **Madeira 6-stranded embroidery floss, one skein each of:**

Dark green 1404	1305 Emerald green
Spring green 1307	0109 Yellow
Scarlet 0210	0601 Maroon
Crimson 0407	0406 Dark salmon
Ssalmon 0303	0304 Pale salmon
Flesh 0305	White

- **Tapestry needle**

- **16 × 16½in backing fabric**

- **15in square pillow form**

This pillow with its beautiful sprays of pink gladioli will make a beautiful complement to the Clematis pillow on pages 17–20. The delicacy of the colors and the subtle blending of the shades in both pillows are achieved in the same way as they might be in a painting. The leaf border is the same design as for the Clematis pillow, although the colors are different to suit the particular colors used for the gladioli. As before, the Latin botanical name of the flowers – in this case, *Iridaceae* – is worked in backstitch in the bottom left-hand corner.

BEFORE YOU BEGIN

Bind or overcast the aida fabric before you start stitching so that it does not fray. The chart for the design is shown opposite. Each square represents one cross-stitch or one three-quarter cross-stitch, and the colors are given in the key. The solid outlines show where to place the backstitching around the outside of the flower petals, leaves, and stems. The inner areas are not defined with back-stitching. The broken lines show where to place the backstitched stamens.

Mark the horizontal and vertical centers of the aida fabric with lines of basting and mark

the chart in pencil to correspond, so that you have guidelines when following the chart. Stretch the fabric in a scroll frame or embroidery hoop to keep it taut as you work; this will give an even tension and a professional finish. The advantage of using a frame is that you can see the whole area of the design as you are stitching. If you use a hoop, you will have to move it around as you work the design.

As some of the colors of the stranded floss are very close in tone, it will be useful to cut lengths of 18in and loop them through the holes on a project card. Write the number and name of the shade beside each one, and you can then easily locate the color you want as you come to it on the chart.

THE GLADIOLI

Begin at the marked center point and stitch the maroon (0601) part of the lower red petal on the large, central gladiolus flower. Use two strands of embroidery floss in the needle for all the cross-stitching. To begin neatly, leave a short length of floss at the back of the fabric and work the first few stitches over it to secure it; to finish off, slip the needle

through the last few stitches worked at the back and cut the end off. In some places, you will need to work three-quarter stitches and quarter stitches to achieve a realistic curved outline (see page 54). On the chart these are indicated where a square is divided diagonally, with one half in one color and the other half in a second color. Work a three-quarter stitch in one of the colors shown and then complete the cross with a quarter stitch in the other color.

Continue stitching the red part of the petal and then move on to the pink shaded part. Take care to choose the right shade of pink as you work from one area to the other, as they are quite close in color. Now work the two red petals bordered with yellow (0109) and then complete the rest of the flower in shades of pink highlighted by white in places. Finish one area of color before moving on to the adjacent one.

Work the remaining gladioli flowers in the same way and, when they are complete, stitch the stems in shades of green, adding the buds tipped with pink.

Now add the backstitched details, using only one strand of floss in the needle. The flower petals are outlined in dark salmon (0406),

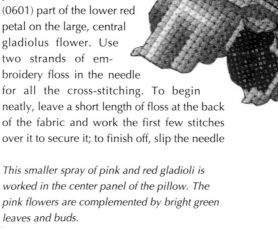

This smaller spray of pink and red gladioli is worked in the center panel of the pillow. The pink flowers are complemented by bright green leaves and buds.

Iridaceae

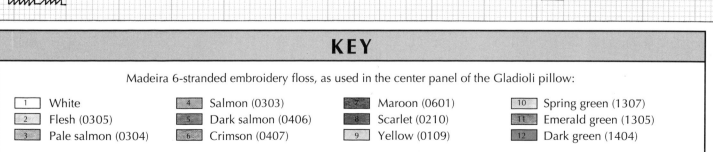

KEY

Madeira 6-stranded embroidery floss, as used in the center panel of the Gladioli pillow:

1 White	4 Salmon (0303)	7 Maroon (0601)	10 Spring green (1307)
2 Flesh (0305)	5 Dark salmon (0406)	8 Scarlet (0210)	11 Emerald green (1305)
3 Pale salmon (0304)	6 Crimson (0407)	9 Yellow (0109)	12 Dark green (1404)

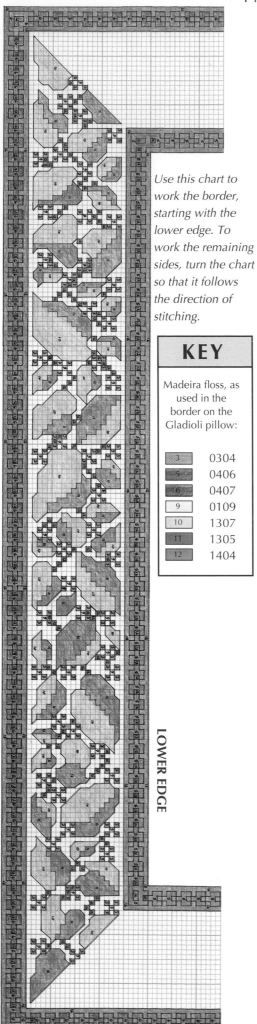

Use this chart to work the border, starting with the lower edge. To work the remaining sides, turn the chart so that it follows the direction of stitching.

KEY

Madeira floss, as used in the border on the Gladioli pillow:

3	0304
5	0406
6	0407
9	0109
10	1307
11	1305
12	1404

LOWER EDGE

while the leaves, buds, and stems are outlined in dark green (1404). Dark green is also the color that is used to stitch the Latin name. The stamens are worked in backstitch in maroon (0601).

ADDING THE LEAF BORDER

The border consists of two geometric bands enclosing a leaf and blossom design. The chart shows one side of the border, which is repeated on all four sides. It also shows you how to turn the corners with the geometric motif. The leaf motifs fit together cleverly at the corners to give a mitered effect.

First work the inner geometric band in dark green and salmon pink, beginning at the lower edge. Count the aida squares carefully from the bottom of the gladioli design to make sure you begin in exactly the right place. If you miscount, the border will not join up correctly. Next stitch the leaves and blossoms, and finally add the outer geometric band in dark green and crimson.

FINISHING THE PILLOW

When you have finished all the embroidery, check that you have not left out any stitches. If necessary, press the work from the wrong side over a padded surface, so you do not

flatten the stitches. Trim the aida fabric to ½in all around and trim the backing fabric to match. Place the two pieces together with right sides facing, and backstitch around three sides, working into the row of holes alongside the border. Leave an opening in the bottom edge. Clip the corners and turn the pillow cover right side out. Insert the pillow form and sew up the opening with neat slipstitches.

bright idea

If you wish, you can repeat areas of the design in the top right and bottom left corners of the center panel. For the top corner, take the top flower and buds from the upper spray and position them 8 squares in from the top and side of the border. For the lower corner, use the top two flowers of the same spray, reverse them, and position them 3 squares in.

Repeat this flower and the spray of buds to fill the top right-hand corner of the center panel.

For the lower left-hand corner, repeat the upper spray again, but this time reverse the motifs. Use the top two flowers and the spray of buds, fitting them neatly around the leaves in the lower spray.

Rose sampler

This traditional cross-stitch alphabet sampler bordered with
vibrant red roses would make a personal and everlasting gift.

Rose sampler

Lovers of roses will appreciate this charming sampler worked in counted cross-stitch. The colors used are fresh and lively, and this gives the roses a velvety, realistic look. The central panel is worked in a classic cross-stitch design, using rows of numbers and alphabets edged with stylized bows and flowers. Embroidered samplers make lovely keepsakes and are a traditional way of marking celebrations and special occasions.

This rose sampler can be personalized by adding a name or a message. The heart at the top edge can be left blank or filled in with intertwining initials taken from the alphabet letters on the chart. The simple frame echoes the natural theme of the sampler, which would look good in any setting.

GOOD WORKING ORDER

The basic rule of working any embroidery picture is to keep the design central by stitching from the middle out: this also helps to avoid distortion of the fabric. Using two strands of floss and following the chart and key, begin with the central alphabet panel. Embroider the red bow using crimson (0210) and scarlet (0513) and then work the border that leads out from the bow using coral (0214) and leaf green (1305). Fill in the wavy line using carnation (0413) and stitch the alphabet in dove gray (1808). Next, work the alphabet and letters at the bottom using dove gray (1808) and soldier blue (1712), before stitching the alphabet at the top in the same colors. Complete the central panel by stitching the pink and red borders at the top and bottom and in between the rows of letters using

carnation (0413), scarlet (0513), crimson (0210), and fern (1502).

BORDER LINES

You are now ready to stitch the rose border. Work one complete area at a time, stopping where there is a natural break in the pattern. For instance, starting at the top left-hand corner, work the corner section consisting of two open roses and two buds, together with their foliage: stitch all the foliage first and then the roses themselves. The greenery is worked in leaf green (1305), apple green (1501), fern (1502) and moss (1314) and the roses in coral (0214), crimson (0210), scarlet (0513), and carnation (0413). Once you have a particular color in your needle, work nearby parts of the design which are the same color. Next stitch the open rose with buds and foliage at the top and bottom. Continue until you have embroidered all around the border.

Finally, stitch the heart at the top in coral (0214) and scarlet (0513) and fill in the geometric outline border using moss (1314) and crimson (0210). Now that the embroidery is complete, you can frame the rose sampler as shown on page 28.

YOU WILL NEED

- **14 × 19in 14-count cream aida fabric**

- **Madeira 6-stranded embroidery floss, one skein each of:**

  Dove gray 1808   1712 Soldier blue
  Apple green 1501   1502 Fern
  Leaf green 1305   1314 Moss
  Carnation 0413   0214 Coral
  Crimson 0210   0513 Scarlet

- **Tapestry needle**

- **Ready-made wooden frame and equipment (see BRIGHT IDEAS and STEPS)**

KEY

Madeira 6-stranded embroidery floss, as used in the Rose sampler:

A	1314	**O**	0214
C	1305	**P**	0413
E	0210	**R**	1502
L	1501	**S**	1712
N	0513	**T**	1808

bright idea

Frames and mats add the finishing touch to a piece of needlework – so select them with care to complement the style of the work being framed. While a specialist framing service will be able to frame the work for you, they also sell everything you need to do the job yourself. An expert will be able to advise you on the different styles and varieties of frame available, and will also be able to help you choose the color and size for a mat and cut it for you if no standard size will fit your work. When you buy your frame, remember to get the correct paper tape and tacks, along with cord for hanging and screw-in hooks to attach it with. You are now ready to put the finishing touch on your work!

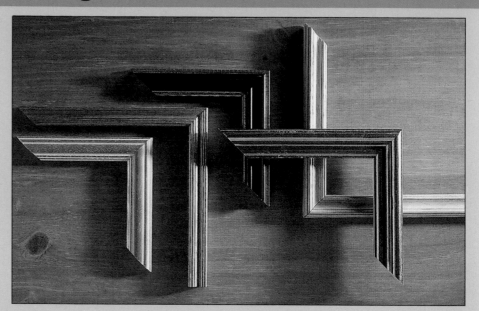

HOW TO FRAME THE SAMPLER

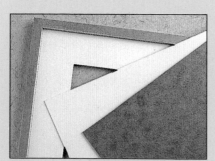

1 Press the sampler, pulling it into shape, then assemble all the parts of your frame and mat along with strong brown-paper tape, thin tacks, a hammer, and masking tape to complete the job.

2 Place the sampler face up on top of the lining board, measuring carefully around all the edges to center the stitched area exactly on the board, so that it can be held in place with masking tape.

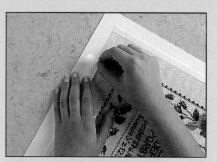

3 Keeping the sampler flat, secure it in place on the lining board using brown-paper tape. Self-adhesive kinds of tape ultimately damage the fabric and should not be used.

4 When the sample is quite smooth, turn the frame face down, and position the mat and the mounted sampler face down in the frame. Add the backing board on top of the lining board.

5 To keep the backing firmly in place, hammer tacks into the inside back of the frame so that they protrude by about 1/8in. Take care not to damage the back with the hammer as you knock in the tacks.

6 To finish the back, use brown-paper tape to mask the edges of the frame, and the backing board. Attach a small screw-in hook on each side of the frame to fix cord for hanging (see box above).

Springtime bouquet

*This glorious array of spring flowers worked in cross-stitch will
bring color into your home all year round.*

Springtime bouquet

Daffodils, irises, tulips, pansies, and polyanthus all feature in this colorful picture, which is a real treat for cross-stitch addicts. The flowers are arranged in pitchers and terracotta pots on a patterned tablecloth just like a still-life painting, and they have been created with all the delicacy of an artist's touch. The clear, fresh colors of stranded floss glow out from the white background. Two shades of floss have been combined in the needle in certain areas to achieve subtle, graduated effects, and extra detail has been added on the tablecloth and some of the flowers with backstitch outlining.

The decorated china pitchers add to the overall pattern and contrast well with the plain brown terracotta flowerpots. The regular print design on the tablecloth has been cleverly arranged to give a softly draped impression to the fabric. The finished picture measures approximately 13½in square.

BEFORE YOU BEGIN

To prevent the raw edges of the fabric from fraying, bind them with masking tape or overcast them before you begin. The design is shown on the chart opposite. Each symbol on the chart equals one cross-stitch, and the solid lines show the backstitched details. The key indicates which colors of stranded floss to use.

Mark the center of the aida fabric horizontally and vertically with lines of basting stitches, and mark the center of the chart in the same way with pencil lines. This will help you to position the stitches when you are following the chart. Mount the fabric in a scroll frame to keep it taut. A frame is preferable to an embroidery hoop for a large picture like this, as it enables you to see the whole picture area at once instead of covering parts of it as you move a hoop around. Also, you can leave the fabric on the frame until the picture is completed instead of having to remove the hoop after each working session.

STITCHING THE DESIGN

Use two strands of floss in the needle for all the cross-stitching, but only one strand for the backstitching. Complete all the cross-stitch areas first, before starting on the backstitching. To secure your thread end when you begin, hold it down at the back of the fabric and work the first few stitches over it; to finish off neatly, slip the thread under the last few stitches at the back and cut the thread end. In this way, loose thread ends do not become caught in subsequent stitching. When you move from one part of the design to another,

YOU WILL NEED

- **20 × 20in 14-count white aida fabric**

- **Madeira 6-stranded embroidery floss, one skein each of:**

Palest yellow 0111	0112 Pale yellow
Lemon yellow 0103	0109 Medium yellow
Buttercup yellow 0108	0114 Pale orange
Bright orange 0202	0106 Bright yellow
Dark crimson 0601	0212 Red
Mauve 0801	0713 Violet
Purple 0714	0503 Light pink
Dark pink 0609	0901 Light blue
Dark lilac 0903	0908 Pale sky blue
Deep sky blue 1012	0911 Cobalt blue
Dark blue 0913	2013 Beige
Brown 2011	0513 Maroon
Amber 2203	1314 Dark green
Light leaf green 1501	1409 Pale green
Leaf green 1502	1410 Lime green
Sage green 1310	1602 Dull green
Terracotta 2306	2007 Dark brown
Pinkish brown 2311	

- **Tapestry needle**

- **Scroll frame**

- **Framing materials**

Pretty mauve irises dominate the top of the picture. Subtle shading is achieved on the flowers by combining dark lilac and dark blue in the needle. The leaves and stems are worked in dark green and dull green to give a more realistic look.

KEY

Madeira 6-stranded embroidery cotton, as used in the Springtime bouquet picture:

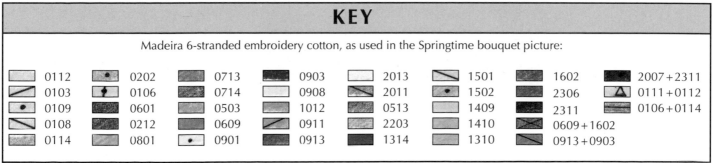

0112	0202	0713	0903	2013	1501	1602	2007 + 2311
0103	0106	0714	0908	2011	1502	2306	0111 + 0112
0109	0601	0503	1012	0513	1409	2311	0106 + 0114
0108	0212	0609	0911	2203	1410	0609 + 1602	
0114	0801	0901	0913	1314	1310	0913 + 0903	

do not take long strands across the back of the work as they can show through at the front and will spoil the finished effect.

Begin stitching centrally with one of the drooping daffodil heads in shades of yellow. Then work the short stem and continue with the rest of the bunch of daffodils, noting that subtle shading is achieved by using one strand each of palest yellow (0111) and pale yellow (0112) combined in the needle. When the daffodils are complete, move on to the irises behind the daffodils. Some of the iris petals are worked with a combination of dark lilac (0903) and dark blue (0913) in the needle. Now work the pink tulips on the right of the irises. These are stitched in two shades of pink, together with a very subtle shading color which is created by combining dark pink (0609) and dull green (1602) in the needle.

When you have finished the tulips and their leaves, work the two pitchers – blue for the daffodils and beige and maroon for the tulips. The pink areas within the maroon pattern on the beige pitcher are worked in light pink (0503). The flowers in the foreground can be stitched next. In the terracotta pots are pansies in two color combinations – yellow with crimson centers and violet and mauve with purple centers. In front of the pots are bright red polyanthus with yellow and green centers and variegated leaves. Finally, work the cross-stitch parts of the patterned tablecloth at the bottom of the picture in deep sky blue (1012), lemon (0103), and amber (2203).

Now that all the cross-stitch parts of the picture are complete, it is time to fill in the

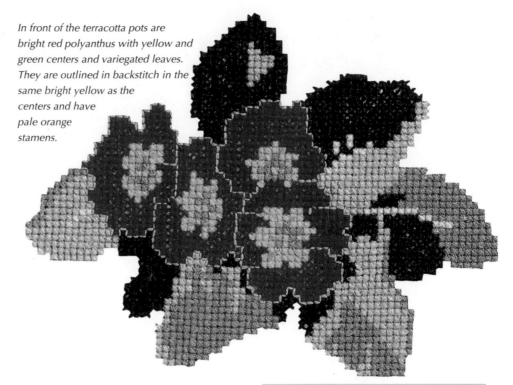

In front of the terracotta pots are bright red polyanthus with yellow and green centers and variegated leaves. They are outlined in backstitch in the same bright yellow as the centers and have pale orange stamens.

backstitch outlines and details. These are shown on the chart as a black line and are worked as follows. Outline some of the daffodil petals in pale orange (0114) to give them definition, and outline some of the tulip leaves in dull green (1602) and dark green (1314). On the violet-colored pansies, add detail to the pale petals with short lines of purple (0714). Outline the polyanthus petals in bright yellow (0106). To finish the picture, outline all the patterned areas of the table-cloth in dark blue (0913), and add extra back-stitched lines at the sides and back of the cloth to extend it to the edges of the picture.

FINISHING THE PICTURE

When the embroidery is complete, check carefully that you have not omitted any stitches and trim any loose ends from the wrong side of the work. Remove the fabric from the frame and press gently from the back over a padded surface so as not to flatten any of the stitches.

Cut a piece of acid-free mat board to measure 13¾in square. Place the embroidery face down on a clean surface and then place the board on the wrong side. Trim the excess fabric to 2in all around. Secure the fabric to the back of the board with masking tape or stretch it over the board by lacing it at the back, cutting away the excess fabric at the corners.

To lace the fabric over the board, use strong sewing thread such as button thread.

be creative

As there are so many areas of interest in this picture, it can be fun to pick some of them out and use them as smaller pieces of embroidery. For example, you could stitch the little bunch of polyanthus on a pincushion, a pair of pansies on a special greeting card, or an array of tulip or daffodil blooms on a make-up bag. You can find the best arrangement by using cardboard L-shapes. To make these, simply cut two L-shaped pieces measuring about 7 × 9in from thin cardboard and position them on the chart or on your finished embroidery in the shape of a frame. You can adjust them until you find an area you like and then reproduce it on 14-count aida in the same way as the main picture.

Start at the center of each side, working up to the top and then down to the bottom. Keep turning the work to the right side to check that it is correctly positioned. When the sides are complete, trim the corners and then fold them into a miter. Lace the top and bottom edges in the same way as for the sides, checking again that the picture is still in the center of the board. Then frame the picture as you wish, either professionally or doing the work yourself.

Thatched cottage

*This thatched cottage with its pretty front yard worked in cross-stitch
is an idyllic view of a perfect rural retreat.*

Thatched cottage

Nestling under a thatched roof and surrounded by a yard bright with country flowers. this cottage is a storybook dream house. The crazy-paving path leading to the front door is edged with herbaceous borders, including such flowers and shrubs as marigolds, pink and blue hydrangeas, irises, stock, lavender, and mallow. Sweet peas climb up the front wall, and the window sill is adorned with little flowerpots. A laburnum tree with its bright yellow, dangling blossoms stands to the left of the cottage, and a birch tree frames the picture on the right. The country cottage is worked entirely in cross-stitch which practically covers the aida, forming a firm, strong fabric with an almost woven look. Only a few areas around the edge of the picture and in the sky are left uncovered.

BEFORE YOU BEGIN

The chart for the cottage picture is shown on the opposite page. Each colored square on the

chart represents one cross-stitch, and the key indicates which shade of yarn to use for each color. The straight lines indicate the back-stitching, which should be worked when all the cross-stitches are complete.

As there are so many different shades of green and brown used in the embroidery, you may find it helpful to organize your stranded floss on project cards. You can make your own by punching holes along the edge of strips of cardboard, then looping 18in lengths of floss through them and writing the shade number and name next to each color. In this way, you will easily be able to find the shade you want as you come to it on the fabric.

To prevent the aida fabric from fraying, bind the edges with masking tape or bias binding. Mark the center of the fabric horizontally and vertically with lines of colored basting which can be removed when the picture is complete. Mark the lines on the chart in pencil to correspond.

There is a great deal of stitching covering the fabric in this design, so you will need to stretch the aida in a scroll frame to prevent the fabric from puckering and to create a smooth, professional-looking result. Using a

frame will also speed up your stitching, as you can work with one hand held above and one below the work.

STITCHING THE COTTAGE

Begin stitching at the center of the fabric, using two strands of floss in the needle. To secure your thread at the beginning, leave a short end at the back and work the first few stitches over it. To finish off neatly, slip the needle under the last few stitches at the back of the work. Take care to snip off all the loose ends as you progress to prevent them from becoming caught in subsequent stitches.

Stitch the framework of the walls first in shades of brown, and then fill in the areas inside the framework. Two shades of yellow – pale yellow (0111) and yellow (0112) – have been dotted around at random to create a mottled look on the wall of the cottage. Add the windows and doors next. The upper windows have bright yellow (0108) curtains with touches of yellow. The lower windows have curtains in sky blue (0908) and pale blue (0901).

Now move up to stitch the thatched roof of the cottage. This is worked in pale coffee

KEY

Madeira 6-stranded embroidery floss, as used in the Thatched cottage picture:

Lime green 1410		Purple 0713	
Gray-green 1401		Brick red 0214	
Dark gray-green 1602		Cerise 0507	
Olive green 1502		Dark brown 2006	
Dark green 1404		Bright yellow 0108	
Sage green 1703		Beige 1910	
Bright green 1307		Bright pink 0414	
Pale mint green 1208		Pale pink 0502	
Mint green 1209		Pale coral 0304	
Jade green 1213		Dark coral 0303	
Pale leaf green 1409		Pale yellow 0111	
Silver gray 1709		Yellow 0112	
Medium gray 1808		Pale copper 2013	
Dark gray 1810		Copper 2011	
Pale blue 0901		Pale coffee 1911	
Medium blue 0906		Coffee 1912	
Sky blue 0908			

STITCH DETAILS

Decorative stitching is worked on top of the cross-stitching on the thatched roof in lines of straight or crossed stitches.

The window of the cottage has a line of colorful little pots of geraniums standing on its sill.

Marigolds and pink hydrangeas are just some of the many flowers in this glorious rural front yard.

brown (1911) and pale copper (2013) and is edged with copper (2011). There are lines of stitching on top of the cross-stitch, just as thatched roofs have decorative tying patterns on them. These are indicated on the chart by solid lines and crossed lines. Use one strand of coffee brown (1912) for these, and work them with long straight stitches or large cross-stitches. To complete the cottage, add the chimneys in brick red (0214) and cerise (0507). Fill in the areas of blue sky above the roof with sky blue, and don't forget the two birds in medium gray (1808).

STITCHING THE YARD

Work the background trees in shades of green with dark brown (2006) trunks. Add the laburnum tree on the left, with its bright yellow blossoms, and the birch tree on the right with its trunk in silver gray (1709) and medium gray and its foliage in three shades of green. Continue by stitching the flowers and shrubs around the cottage. The sweet peas in front of the house are pale pink (0502) and bright pink (0414), and the stocks at the far right of the picture are pale coral (0304), dark coral (0303), and pale yellow. The hydrangeas at the front of the right-hand bed are worked in three shades of blue, and the other flowers behind them are in brick red and cerise.

The marigolds in the left-hand bed are worked in bright yellow and brick red, while the mallow shrub has bright pink and cerise

flowers with medium blue centers. In front of this shrub are irises in two shades of blue with purple and yellow, and also another hydrangea bush in two shades of pink. The foliage is worked in a variety of greens. Finally, fill in the path in silver gray and medium gray.

Some details in the picture, such as flower stems and the birds' wings, have been added in backstitch when the cross-stitching is complete. These are shown by colored solid lines on the chart and are worked in backstitch using one strand of floss in the needle.

FINISHING THE PICTURE

Remove the embroidery from the frame and press lightly from the wrong side over a lightly padded surface if necessary. Mount and frame the picture as you wish.

bright idea

Some of the flowers in the well-stocked beds and borders would make pretty decorative motifs in their own right. Here we have isolated the purple and blue irises to stitch for a greeting card. To do this, look at the key and then use leftover lengths of the colors indicated to work this portion of the design in cross-stitch, omitting the green background. When the stitching is complete, make a card as described on page 125.

Cute kittens

This pretty cross-stitch design of two tabby kittens with bows around their necks is reminiscent of Berlin woolwork pictures.

Cute kittens

KEY

Madeira 6-stranded embroidery floss, as used in the Cute kittens:

	0414		0810
╱	0610		1801
	0507		1804
	1604	○	1905
•	1502	╱	1910
	0209		2006
	0503		2009
	1501		2011
	1608		2013
	0908		1911
	0907	•	2101
✕	1012	✕	2203
	0106	✚	2312
	0114		Black
	0809		White

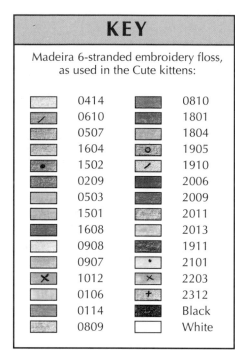

These two little tabby kittens, sitting on a checked pillow, are so realistic that you will want to pick them up and take them home. They both have pastel-colored bows around their necks, and a red geranium fills one corner of the picture.

The kittens' intricate shading is created by using Madeira 6-stranded embroidery floss in a wide range of browns and golds with highlights in white and gray. A tortoiseshell-effect frame and a cream mat complete the design, but these can be changed to suit any room setting of your choice.

BEFORE YOU START

Bind the edges of the aida fabric with either masking tape or bias binding to prevent them from fraying as you stitch. If you use masking tape, make sure that it is wide enough to cover the edges securely and that it is well stuck down onto the fabric. Fold the aida fabric lightly in half and half again and mark the center horizontal and vertical lines with basting. Use sewing thread which can be worked over and removed when the design is complete. Mark the corresponding center point on the color chart opposite with a pencil.

Mount the fabric in an embroidery hoop or scroll frame if you wish. This will keep it taut as you work and ensure that all your stitching is of an even tension. If you use a hoop, great care must be taken when moving it around the fabric so that none of the previously worked stitching becomes damaged. A sheet of acid-free tissue paper placed between the aida fabric and the hoop may help to prevent this

– it will also help to keep the fabric clean around the edges of the hoop.

There are several shades of brown used to work the kitten design. Fasten 18in lengths of each color on a project card and label them clearly with their skein numbers to help identify them more easily when you reach them on the chart.

STITCHING THE DESIGN

Each colored square on the chart equals one cross-stitch, which is worked using two strands of embroidery floss in the needle. Follow the key on the left for the colors to use. Always finish one area of stitching before moving on to the next, and avoid passing long strands of floss across the back of the work as they may become caught in subsequent stitching and cause the back of the work to become tangled. If this happens, the picture may be difficult to mount and frame.

YOU WILL NEED

- **14 × 16in 14-count cream aida fabric**

- **Madeira 6-stranded embroidery floss, one skein each of:**

Pale pink 0503	0507 Deep pink
Orange 0209	0908 Pale blue
Blue 0907	1501 Lime green
Bright green 1502	1608 Olive green
Yellow 0106	0114 Yellow-gold
Sky blue 1012	0414 Sugar pink
Dusty rose 0809	0810 Dark rose
Dark green 1404	1801 Dark gray
Pale gray 1804	1905 Taupe
Beige 1910	2006 Dark brown
Gold-brown 2011	2013 Medium beige
Tan brown 2009	1911 Taupe
Cream 2101	2203 Green-gold
Pink-brown 2312	0610 Pink
Pale green 1604	Black
	White

- **Tapestry needle**

This little kitten, with its pretty pink bow, is worked on the left-hand side of the picture. It has blue eyes and a soft pink nose. The dark browns and gold used for the kitten's head are contrasted by its white chest stripes.

Never start stitching with a knot; leave a short end on the wrong side and work over it with the first few stitches. To finish the work off neatly, slip the needle back through a few stitches. At this point, work all the cross-stitching only, leaving the backstitch details until the design is complete.

Starting at the marked center points on both the fabric and the chart, begin stitching the right-hand kitten's leg. When this is complete, move on to stitch its face and body. Work the very small areas of color, such as the eyes and mouth, first and then fill in the larger areas around them. In this way you are less likely to make a mistake. When you have finished stitching the kitten, work its bow using three shades of blue.

For the brown-and-white kitten on the left, start by stitching the areas that adjoin those already worked for the beige kitten, stitching from the center of the fabric toward the edges. Once again, end with the kitten's bow, which is worked in three shades of pink.

Once the two kittens are complete, stitch the checked cushion around them. This is worked in green with a slightly darker shade for the shadows, and has a trellis pattern in dusty rose and deep pink. Finally, work the red geranium plant in the top right-hand corner. The flower petals are worked in red and pink and have soft blue centers. Before you move on to work the backstitching, check that you have not missed any cross-stitches, as these will be difficult to add at a later stage.

BACKSTITCH DETAILS

Use two strands of floss in the needle for all the backstitching except the kittens' whiskers, which are worked with only one strand. Starting at the top right-hand corner of the picture, work the details on the geranium flower petals in deep pink (0507). This color is also used to work the details on the pink bow. The leaf veins should be worked in dark green (1404); note that this is the only time that this color is used.

Next, use sky blue (1012) to work the backstitching on the blue bow. To outline the beige kitten's paw and ear, use dark brown (2006). The kittens' mouths are worked in dark gray (1801).

When you come to work the kittens' whiskers, use only one strand of dark brown floss in the needle and work them in free backstitch. To work this, follow the lines marked on the chart, but do not necessarily follow the holes of the aida fabric as you normally would. Working through the center of some stitches as well will help you to

achieve a softer, curved line of stitching. Take care, though, that you still keep the stitches short and neat in the way you would if you were following the holes in the aida fabric.

FINISHING TOUCHES

Remove the embroidery from the hoop or frame and press the design carefully from the wrong side over a lightly padded surface. This will prevent the stitches from becoming flattened. Mount and frame the picture as required. If you use a mat board, check that it is acid-free or it may cause a discoloration of the fabric over a period of time.

STITCH DETAILS

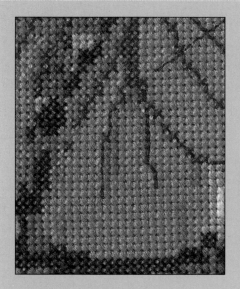

Three shades of pink are used to work the brown-and-white kitten's bow, which is also backstitched in deep pink. This is a perfect contrast to the dark fur.

The brown-and-white kitten has bright blue eyes with black and white pupils. Just below these features are worked a small pink nose and a smiling gray mouth.

For the beige tabby kitten, a variety of lighter browns and taupes has been used for the fur. This is highlighted with splashes of medium gray floss.

Deer in the heather

Set against a magnificent Highland backdrop, these deer make a splendid subject for a cross-stitch picture.

YOU WILL NEED

- 14½ × 16½in 14-count cream aida fabric

- Madeira 6-stranded embroidery floss, one skein each of:

Beige 2011	2009 Medium tan
Tan 2008	2007 Brown
Cream 2101	0706 Fuchsia
Pink 0708	0710 Pale pink
Leaf green 1502	1501 Pale leaf green
Taupe 1912	1905 Gray brown
Sage green 1602	1310 Pale sage green
Dark green 1314	1605 Spring green
Mauve 0801	Black

- Tapestry needle

- Scroll frame

- Acid-free mat board

Deer picture

Two deer and a fawn make up this peaceful group in a Highland setting. Purple heather adds a splash of color in the foreground, echoed by the mauve of the distant mountain range. Evergreen branches frame the top of the picture on either side, and a fallen tree trunk lies behind the deer. Worked in cross-stitch and backstitch, the picture measures 10 × 12½in. Framed with a dark wood or gilt frame, it would look effective in a traditional setting in a living room or study, and would make a wonderful present for a conservationist or animal-loving friend.

BEFORE YOU BEGIN

To prevent fraying, bind the raw edges of the aida fabric with bias binding or masking tape or overcast them. Mark the center of the fabric horizontally and vertically with lines of basting; mark the center of the chart in pencil in the same way. This will give you a guide when you begin to stitch from the chart.

The chart for the deer design is shown on the opposite page. Each colored square equals one cross-stitch and the solid lines show the backstitched

details. The key indicates which colors of stranded floss are to be used. To give a subtle, slightly mottled effect to some parts of the picture, two colors of stranded floss have been used together in the needle. Where this happens, both colors are listed side by side in the key.

For a professional-looking result, mount the fabric in a scroll fame; this keeps it taut while you are stitching and makes it easier to see the picture growing as you follow the chart. If you use an embroidery hoop, you will need to move it around the fabric as you progress. Protect stitched areas with tissue paper before tightening a hoop over them, and remove the hoop after each work session to avoid marking the fabric permanently. If you begin stitching at the center and then work the top of the picture before the bottom, you are less likely to snag stitches or make them grubby.

As there are many shades of brown and green in this design, you will find it helpful to sort your stranded floss on project cards so that you can locate each color easily as you need it. You can either make your own by punching a row of holes along the side of a strip of cardboard, or you can buy them ready-made. Cut the floss into working lengths of about 18in and loop them through the holes. Write the shade name and number beside each one.

STITCHING THE PICTURE

Use two strands of floss in the needle for all the cross-stitching. To secure the thread at the beginning, leave a short end at the back and work the first few stitches over it; to finish your work off neatly, thread the needle through the last few stitches at the back and trim the end.

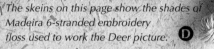

The skeins on this page show the shades of Madeira 6-stranded embroidery floss used to work the Deer picture.

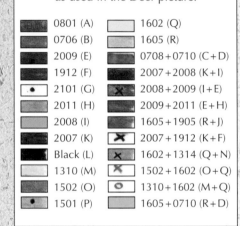

KEY

Madeira 6-stranded embroidery floss, as used in the Deer picture:

▦	0801 (A)	▦	1602 (Q)
▦	0706 (B)	▦	1605 (R)
▦	2009 (E)	▦	0708+0710 (C+D)
▦	1912 (F)	▦	2007+2008 (K+I)
⊡	2101 (G)	✕	2008+2009 (I+E)
▦	2011 (H)	▦	2009+2011 (E+H)
▦	2008 (I)	▦	1605+1905 (R+J)
▦	2007 (K)	✕	2007+1912 (K+F)
■	Black (L)	✕	1602+1314 (Q+N)
▦	1310 (M)	✕	1502+1602 (O+Q)
▦	1502 (O)	⊙	1310+1602 (M+Q)
⊡	1501 (P)	▦	1605+0710 (R+D)

Following the chart, begin stitching at the center with the largest deer. Very subtle shading is achieved by using a wide variety of browns and mixing two different shades together in the needle in some places. Where you need to use mixed colors, use one strand of each in the needle. Work one area of color at a time, and do not carry long strands across the back of the fabric as these can get caught in subsequent stitching.

The twisted skeins on the left show the shades of brown that are used to work the deer and the surrounding trees. On the right are the shades of green that are needed. The shades of pink and mauve are shown above right.

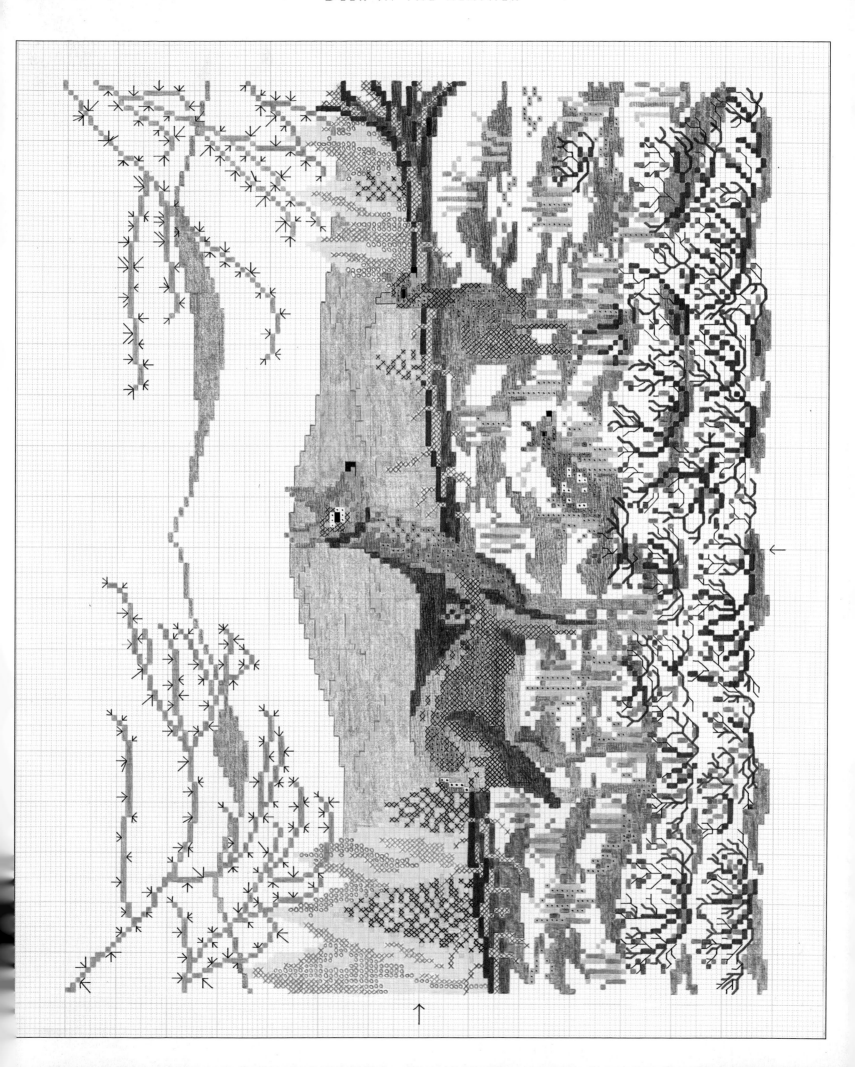

When the first deer is complete, stitch the fallen tree trunk behind it in brown (2007) and taupe (1912), combining these two colors in some areas. Then work the smaller standing deer in browns and tans as for the first deer. Moving up, stitch the mountain in the background by combining spring green (1605) and pale pink (0710) in the needle. Add some areas of spring green to show foliage. Stitch the trees on each side of the picture in sage green (1602), pale sage green (1310), dark green (1314), and leaf green (1502), again combining strands in some places. Long evergreen branches come into the picture at the top; work these next, but leave the backstitched needles until later. Then add the far-distant mountain range in mauve.

In foreground of the picture, begin to fill in the heather foliage around the deer, adding the fawn when you reach it on the chart. The heather foliage is worked in spring green (1605), pale leaf green (1501), leaf green (1502), and taupe, with some mottled areas in spring green combined with gray brown (1905). Add the heather flowers in shades of pink and fuchsia.

THE FINAL TOUCHES

When all the cross-stitching is complete, add the backstitched details. Use two strands of floss in the needle for these. The smaller standing deer's ears are outlined in tan (2008) and its eye in cream (2101), as is the fawn's

A large deer stands guard over the smaller deer and fawn. The fur is worked in shades of brown, with some of the colors created by blending a strand of two different colors in the needle.

eye. The deers' mouths are backstitched using black floss. The finer heather stalks in the foreground of the chart are worked in leaf green (1502), and the thicker ones in taupe. The larch needles are a combination of leaf green and spring green. To complete the backstitching, work the details on the hill in the background using sage green (1602).

FINISHING THE PICTURE

When the embroidery is complete, remove it from the frame or hoop. Check carefully that you have not left out any stitches as these will be difficult to add once the picture has been framed. Trim off any loose ends at the back which might show through at the front when the picture is mounted.

Press the embroidery carefully on the wrong side over a padded surface to prevent the stitches from being flattened. Cut a piece of mat board to the required size. Trim the excess fabric from around the design so that it is just 1¼in bigger than the mat board. Stretch the fabric over the board and secure on the wrong side with brown-paper tape. Mount and frame the picture as required (see page 28).

STITCH DETAILS

The deer's features are delicately depicted in subtle shades of brown with some backstitch details.

The heather flowers are worked in vivid pinkish purples, and the stalks are backstitched for a realistic look.

A variety of sage greens is used for the evergreens, and different colored strands are combined in some places.

Harbor view

*Keep memories of vacations by the ocean fresh with
this evocative harbor scene worked in cross-stitch.*

Harbor view

YOU WILL NEED

- **10½ × 12in 14-count white aida fabric**

- **Madeira 6-stranded embroidery floss, one skein each of:**

Indigo blue 0903	0905 Dark blue
Blue 0907	0908 Turquoise blue
Pale blue 0901	1404 Dark green
Olive green 1608	1810 Dark brown
Gray brown 1808	2008 Tan
Mauve gray 1806	0210 Scarlet
Black	White

- **Tapestry needle**

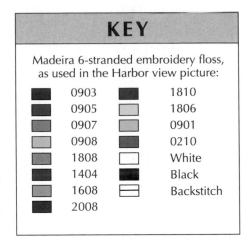

KEY

Madeira 6-stranded embroidery floss, as used in the Harbor view picture:

■	0903	■	1810
■	0905	▨	1806
■	0907	▨	0901
▨	0908	■	0210
■	1808	□	White
■	1404	■	Black
■	1608	⊟	Backstitch
■	2008		

Whether you are lucky enough to live on the coast or whether you live far inland, you'll find this picture of a harbor scene very enjoyable to stitch. The sea is worked in different shades of blue for a lively effect on the rather choppy waves, and the sky has billowing clouds. The little houses at the harbor's edge are delicately depicted, and the boats in the foreground add a sense of movement.

Worked in cross-stitch on 14-count aida fabric, the picture measures 6¼ × 7¾in when complete. Unlike many cross-stitch designs, much of the surface of the aida is covered with stitching so that little is left showing. Backstitches worked in a single strand of floss add the finishing touches. Add a contrasting mat and a classic wooden frame to complete the picture.

BEFORE YOU START

Mark the center of your fabric with lines of colored basting thread. Mount the fabric in a scroll frame if you wish. Use two strands of floss in the needle, taking each strand from the length of thread and then re-combining them to give a smooth appearance to your work.

Begin by leaving a length of thread at the back of the work and working the first few stitches over it to secure it. Finish by running the thread under the last few stitches at the back of the work.

Remember that all the top legs of the cross-stitches should lie in the same direction for a professional-looking finish. Trim off any loose ends as you stitch as they may become caught in subsequent stitching and cause an unsightly finish on the right side of the work.

WORKING THE STITCHING

Work the design following the chart opposite. Each square on the chart represents one cross-stitch, with the key showing which colors to use. The design is worked in cross-stitch throughout except for a few details which are added in backstitch at the end.

Begin by stitching the lighthouse using white floss, and the cliffs behind it using shades of brown. Working out from this point, stitch the row of houses and the harbor wall. When you are working the houses, you may find it easier to work the windows and small details first and then build the rest of the houses around them. This will also help to catch down any short ends that result from working small areas of stitching.

The next step is to work the small red boat in the foreground and the green boat on the right of the harbor wall. Once these are

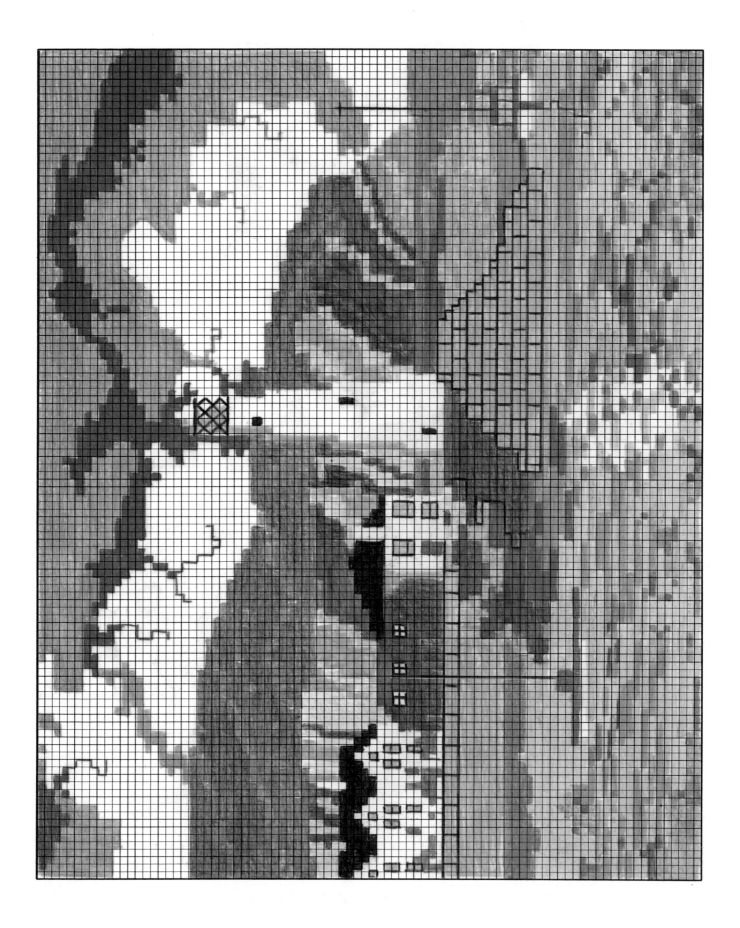

STITCH DETAILS

Add an extra dimension to this little row of fishermen's houses by working single-strand black backstitches around the windows and using dark green for the shrubs.

Using two strands of black floss, work backstitches in a diamond pattern to form the lantern at the top of the lighthouse. Work a straight line at the top and bottom.

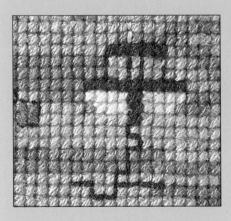

Here, single-strand green backstitches are used to create a ripple in the water in front of the small green boat, giving the water a more realistic feel.

Careful shading can make a great deal of difference on large expanses of color. Use shades of brown and gray to give depth to the cliff face behind the town.

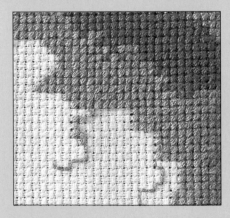

The clouds in the sky are the only areas in the picture not completely covered with stitching. Use backstitching to create billows.

When you are working the grassy knoll above the cliff face, work the green lines first and then fill in with dark green.

complete, work the sea. As before, you may find it easier to work the small areas of color first to give you a reference point.

When the sea is complete, work the grassy knoll above the cliff face. Start by working the green hill lines and shadow, and then fill in around them with the dark green. The last element to work is the sky. Use the area around the tip of the lighthouse as a starting point and work outward.

FINISHING TOUCHES

When all the cross-stitching is complete, work the backstitch details. Use one strand of black floss to outline the cottage windows and the stones in the harbor wall, and to make an anchor chain for the red boat. The masts of the two boats are worked using one strand of white floss – these will show up clearly against the darker shades of stranded floss behind them. Work the ripples in the water in front of the green boat using one strand of dark green.

Complete the lighthouse by working a diamond pattern at the top, using two strands of black floss. Finish the top and bottom edges with a straight line. For a final detail, work single-strand backstitches in the two blues used for the sky to create curved clouds.

When the picture is complete, remove it from the frame and press it on the wrong side over a padded surface. If your work has become dirty during stitching, you may wish to wash it carefully before it is framed. Use lukewarm water and a nonbiological detergent, rinse well, then pin it out loosely in shape and dry flat. Again, always press from the wrong side over a padded surface.

bright idea

Give this picture a real nautical feel with a clever choice of frame. Sea shells collected on beach vacations can easily be set into ceramic tile adhesive to create an interesting border. The more shells you use, the more unusual the finished effect will be, but avoid very large shells which will make the finished frame very heavy. Glue the shells onto an old frame or cut a square window mat from a piece of wood. Whatever you use, check first that it will take the weight of the shells.

Hollyhocks

*Butterflies hovering above tall hollyhocks make this
an ideal card for a summer birthday.*

Hollyhock card

Hollyhocks are among the most impressive of flowers and make the perfect subject for this summery card worked in cross-stitch. Two butterflies hovering above the tall blooms add a light-hearted touch.

The stranded embroidery floss is in luscious shades of pink, lilac, violet, and orange for the flowers, set off by two shades of green for the variegated foliage. The design is worked on white 14-count aida fabric.

STITCHING THE CARD

Use two strands of floss in the needle to work the cross-stitch. The chart for the floral design is shown on the right. Each colored symbol represents one cross-stitch worked over one block of the aida fabric.

Find the center of the fabric by creasing it gently horizontally and vertically. You can run lines of colored basting thread along the creases to mark the center if you wish. Then begin by stitching the central hollyhock. Make sure that the top half of each cross-stitch always slants in the same direction; otherwise, the embroidery will look messy. Use light green for the leaves, and lilac and violet for the flowers. Complete the flowers by adding dark pink centers. Next work the foreground

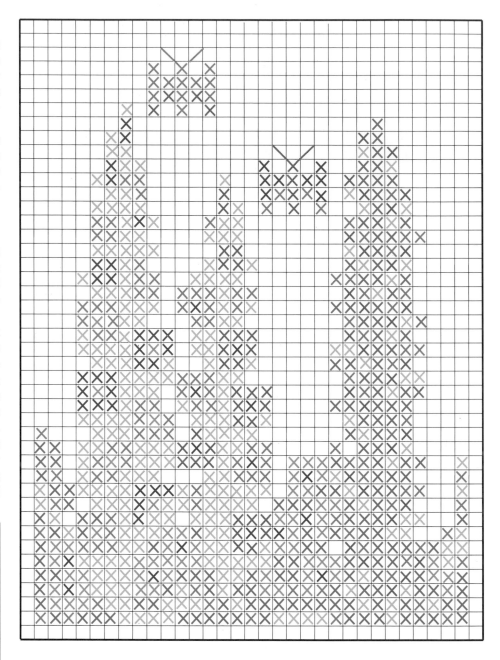

YOU WILL NEED

- **3 × 4in 14-count white aida fabric**

- **Madeira 6-stranded embroidery floss, one skein each of:**

  Light green 1409   0809 Lilac
  Violet 0902   0406 Dark pink
  Orange 2307   1609 Green
  Pink 0405

- **Tapestry needle**

- **Pre-cut card and envelope**

- **Fabric glue**

flowers in orange with dark pink centers, adding single crosses of pink here and there as highlighting. The foliage around the flowers is green and light green.

Work the flowers on the left-hand hollyhock in pink and dark pink with orange centers. The leaves are light green. The right-hand hollyhock has lilac and pink flowers and its leaves are worked in both shades of green. Finally add the two butterflies, working their feelers with straight stitches.

FINISHING THE CARD

Trim the fabric to fit the center fold of the card. Cover the back side of the central section of the card mount sparingly with fabric glue and lay it over the embroidery, making sure that the design is correctly positioned inside the "window."

Glue the back of the front flap around the edges and fold it over the fabric, pressing down firmly to seal it (see also instructions for "Making a greeting card" on page 125).

Go fly a kite

On a birthday or friendship card, this bright-colored kite looks jolly, flying with streaming bows amid the clouds.

The kite is worked in cross-stitch with the tail and streamers worked in backstitch.

Kite card

needle, but the tail, ribbons, and birds are worked using only one strand. This gives your card a delicate finish.

After you have finished working the kite and the clouds in cross-stitch, work the kite's tail and ribbons in backstitch. The three birds are made of two backstitches in a V-shape.

FINISHING THE CARD

To finish the card, trim the fabric evenly to measure $3\frac{1}{4} \times 4$in. For easy step-by-step instructions on how to mount your work in a card, see the instructions for "Making a greeting card" on page 125.

see the instructions for "Making a greeting card" on page 125.

YOU WILL NEED

- **$3\frac{1}{4} \times 4$in 14-count white aida fabric**
- **Madeira 6-stranded embroidery floss, one skein each of:**

  Red 0507 0307 Orange
  Green 1203 0908 Gray blue
  Yellow 0109

- **Tapestry needle**
- **Pre-cut card and envelope**
- **Fabric glue**

N o one is too old to fly a kite on a windy day, and this little card with its bright ribbon streamer will be sure to remind you of family days out. The card is suitable for all ages from small children to adults and can be used for a variety of special occasions.

TO STITCH THE CARD

Begin by finding the center of your aida fabric. To do this, fold the fabric so that the creases cross in the middle. The design is worked in cross-stitch and backstitch.

Mark the center of the chart in pencil and begin stitching at the centerpoint on the fabric. First work the four main colors of the kite's body using cross-stitch. Each cross on the chart represents one stitch and shows the colors to use. The kite and the clouds are worked using two strands of floss in the

---

HANDY

When you are working small areas of color, such as the kite's tail, you may not want to pass the embroidery floss across the back of the work. You can finish off on the wrong side by making two or three small buttonhole stitches over one of the stitches. Take care not to pull this stitch too tight or it will distort the right side of the work.

HINT

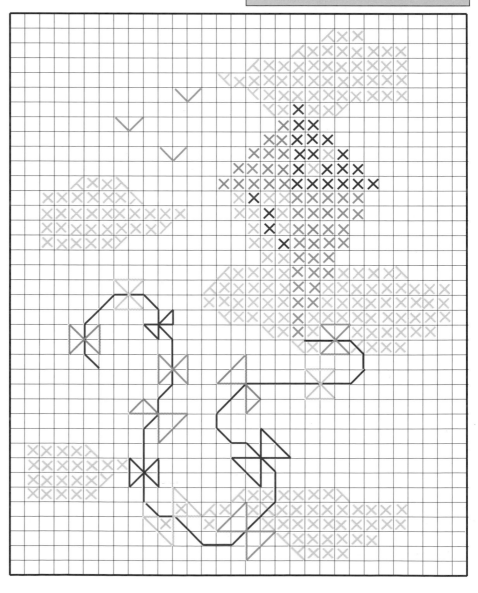

Let's celebrate!

Champagne is a stylish way to celebrate an occasion – and what better way to
congratulate a friend than a hand-stitched card complete with bubbles?

QUARTER CROSS-STITCH

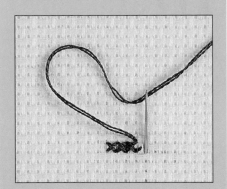

For a three-quarter cross-stitch which slopes down to the right, make the first part of the stitch from the center of the intersection of aida threads, then stitch as normal when you add the crossing stitch.

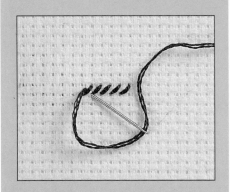

For a three-quarter stitch which slopes down to the left, stitch the first leg of the stitch as normal, then bring the thread up in the intersection of the aida threads, then complete the stitch as normal.

Celebration card

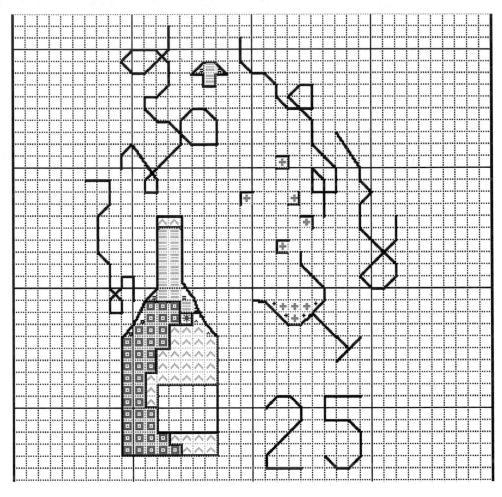

In the chart above, one colored cross represents one cross-stitch. Stitch the straight lines and numbers (see page 125) in backstitch.

For a birthday or anniversary, this card will fit the bill. Just change the numbers to suit the occasion.

First, mark the center of the fabric and stretch it in a small embroidery hoop. Start by working on the bottle below center to the left. Work in two strands of floss.

Follow the chart, shaping with three-quarter stitches where shown as smaller symbols. For how to work three-quarter cross-stitch, see the steps above. Work the streamers in backstitch in pink and blue and the outlines in one strand of black.

Select the numbers you need from the stitched example on page 125, position them as on the chart, and work them first in two strands of pink in Holbein stitch, or backstitch, and then repeat using blue floss.

Finally, press the embroidery from the wrong side and mount it in the card as shown on page 125.

PRACTICAL

You can stitch names and dates on your designs to add a personal touch. To work out the shapes and positions of the letters and numbers you wish to use, draw them on graph paper from an alphabet chart, or create your own. When you are happy with the placement, find the center of the area on your graphed chart and on your fabric, and stitch your message.

POINT

YOU WILL NEED

- **3 × 4in 18-count white aida fabric**

- **Madeira 6-stranded embroidery floss, one skein each of:**

  Dark green 0890   0701 Emerald green
  Yellow 0726   0798 Blue
  Pink 0309   0754 Pale peach
  Black

- **Tapestry needle**

- **Pre-cut card and envelope**

- **Fabric glue**

Be my Valentine!

Combine traditional symbols of hearts and doves on this simple cross-stitch card to create the perfect Valentine.

Valentine card

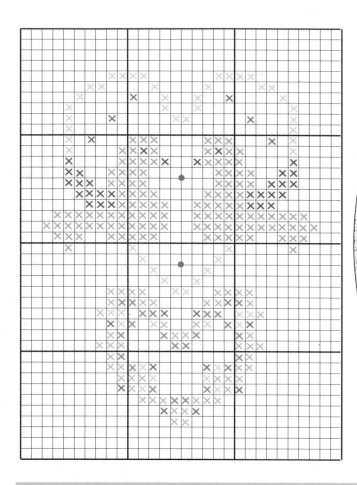

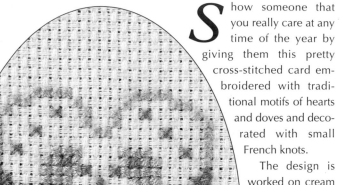

Show someone that you really care at any time of the year by giving them this pretty cross-stitched card embroidered with traditional motifs of hearts and doves and decorated with small French knots.

The design is worked on cream 14-count aida fabric using two strands of floss throughout.

Follow the chart, with each stitch covering one square of the fabric, and work your way out from the central point. This can be marked by folding the aida in half horizontally and then vertically. Start with the body of the birds in the light blue, moving out to their wings, which are darker blue, and then work the large heart around them using the pale pink. Stitch the smaller heart using both greens and pinks. Complete the design by working dark pink French knots (see page 109) as marked by a dot on the chart.

To make the card, see page 125.

STITCHING THE DESIGN

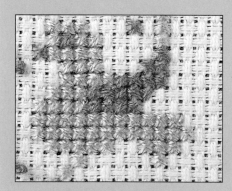

Stitch the bodies of the doves in light blue and then work their wings in a darker blue – you may find it easier to work the bodies first. The wings are given a curved outline underneath by working one three-quarter cross-stitch at the end of the second row, starting from the bottom of the wing (see page 54).

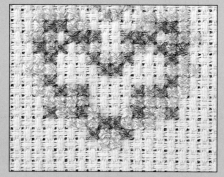

To work the green and pink heart, stitch each color separately, starting with the lighter pink. Make sure all the top diagonals of the crosses lie in the same direction to produce small, neat crosses. It is helpful to secure each thread end before moving on to the next color so that the threads do not tangle.

YOU WILL NEED

- 3 × 4in 14-count cream aida fabric
- Madeira 6-stranded embroidery floss, one skein each of:

  Pale blue 0901   1012 Dark blue
  Pale pink 0503   0609 Dark pink
  Pale green 1209   1203 Dark green

- Tapestry needle
- Pre-cut oval card & envelope
- Fabric glue

Merry Christmas!

*Make someone feel special at Christmas with
a hand-embroidered card in traditional festive colors.*

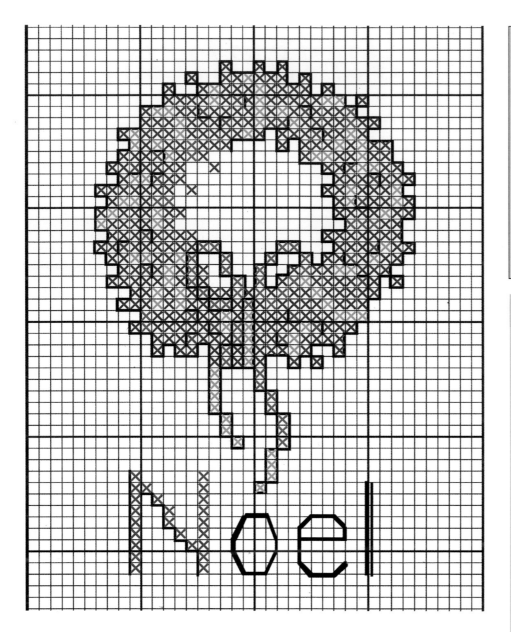

YOU WILL NEED

- **3 × 4in 18-count white aida fabric**
- **Madeira 6-stranded embroidery cotton, one skein each of:**

  Dark green 1304   0906 Light green
  Yellow 0108   0308 Orange
  Red 0510   2008 Brown

- **Tapestry needle**
- **Pre-cut card and envelope**
- **Fabric glue**

FINISHING TOUCHES

1 *Add a gold outline for a personal touch. Using a gold marker pen, draw a gold line around the grooved side edges of the card's frame, taking care not to overrun the corners.*

2 *An alternative creative touch is to fill in the whole inner frame in gold. Carefully draw around the inside edge of the frame with a gold marker pen, keeping within the parallel lines. This will add a mark of distinction to your card.*

Christmas card

Bright holly berries and yellow ribbons add seasonal color to the wreath on this card, It is worked in counted cross-stitch using two strands of embroidery floss, except for the outline and the details on the ribbon and berries, which are worked in one strand of brown thread.

Before you start, mark the center of your fabric. Begin working in dark green to the right of the yellow ribbon which hangs from the bow. Complete one section of dark green at a time, adding the ribbon in yellow and orange after each one, until you have filled in all eight sections. Now add the holly berries and light green foliage. Add the bow, then, using one strand of brown, work all around the outer and inner edges of the wreath, the bow, and the hanging ribbons in Holbein stitch (see page 82). Finally, stitch the letter N in cross-stitch and the remaining letters in Holbein stitch in two strands of red, adding a shading line in a single strand of brown.

FINISHING THE CARD
To make the card, follow the directions on page 125.

Tile sachet

*This pretty little cross-stitch potpourri holder would be
a welcome addition to any closet.*

Tile sachet

YOU WILL NEED

- **4 × 4in 14-count cream aida fabric**
- **Madeira 6-stranded embroidery floss, one skein each of:**

  Bright blue 0903   1712 Dark blue
  Light green 1605   1602 Dark green
  Rust 2306   2011 Beige

- **Tapestry needle**
- **4 × 4in backing fabric**
- **Cream sewing thread**
- **Sharps needle**
- **2½in cream ribbon, ⅛in wide**
- **Potpourri for filling**

What better way to keep the clothes in your closet or chest of drawers smelling sweet than with this Victorian-style potpourri sachet?

STITCHING THE DESIGN

Fold the aida fabric in half both ways and crease lightly to find the center. If you wish, overcast the edges of the aida fabric to prevent them from fraying as you stitch. Using two strands of floss, begin stitching centrally by working four cross-stitches in beige. Complete the inner part of the design by working the large blue flower and the pale green leaves. Now work the beige border of cross-stitches and outline them in rust backstitches. The blue flowers in the corners of the inner frame should be worked next, followed by the dark green border. The outer border is worked in beige with rust backstitching to match the square frame in the center of the design.

Complete the potpourri sachet with an outer edging of dark blue cross-stitches. Once all the cross-stitching is complete, work the backstitch details that finish the design, such as the

This pretty potpourri sachet with its center square and concentric floral patterns is worked in cross-stitch and backstitch using the same colors as the Mirror case on page 61.

flower stems and leaves. Follow the chart above, working with two strands of floss in the needle.

FINISHING THE SACHET

Press the design lightly on the wrong side over a padded surface to prevent the stitches from becoming flattened. Fold the ribbon in half and, matching the raw edges to those on the fabric, pin it securely to one corner of the sachet. Place the finished design and the backing fabric together with right sides facing. Use matching sewing thread to backstitch around three sides, securing the ends of the ribbon in the seam.

Clip across the corners of the seam to remove the excess fabric and turn the work right side out. Lightly fill the sachet with small pieces of potpourri. Turn under the raw edges along the embroidered stitches and slipstitch the remaining side to close.

Tile mirror case

Make this pretty case to protect your mirror
and keep it safe in your purse.

Tile mirror case

YOU WILL NEED

- **4 × 4in 14-count cream aida fabric**
- **Madeira 6-stranded embroidery floss, one skein each of:**

  Beige 2011   2306 Rust

  Dark blue 1712   1602 Dark green

  Light green 1605   0903 Bright blue

- **Tapestry needle**
- **4 × 10½in lining fabric**
- **White sewing thread**
- **Sharps needle**

This mirror case is decorated with oak leaves and flowers and has an autumnal feel. The aida design is backed and lined with a cotton blend to create a protective pouch. The finished case measures 3¼in square.

STITCHING THE DESIGN

Find the centers of the fabric and the chart. Work the design in cross-stitch using two strands of floss in the needle. Stitch all of the cross-stitches first and then add the scrolling backstitch.

Follow the chart above to work the design. Each symbol represents one cross-stitch and shows the color to use. Begin by stitching the heart-shaped motifs in the center of the mirror case and continue working out from there. The corners of the flowers and leaves are worked in three-quarter cross-stitch. When the cross-stitches are complete, work the backstitching using one strand of floss in the needle.

FINISHING THE CASE

Press the embroidery on the wrong side over a padded surface. Cut the piece of lining fabric in half, with each piece the same size as the aida fabric. Place the embroidery face down on the lining fabric and, using the sewing thread, backstitch around three sides of the two pieces, leaving the top edge open. Turn right side out. Fold the remaining piece of lining fabric in half

widthwise and backstitch the two sides to create a lining. Insert the lining into the mirror case. Turn under the seam allowance along the top edges and slipstitch to secure.

HANDY

When you are working three-quarter cross-stitches, you may find it easier to achieve a neat finish if you work the short "legs" of the stitch, which only cover one half of the aida square, first. Then when you work the second, longer "leg" of the stitch, the hole made by the first leg in the center of the square will be covered.

HINT

Pinwheel needlecase

This little needlecase is very quick to stitch and will prove invaluable in your sewing box.

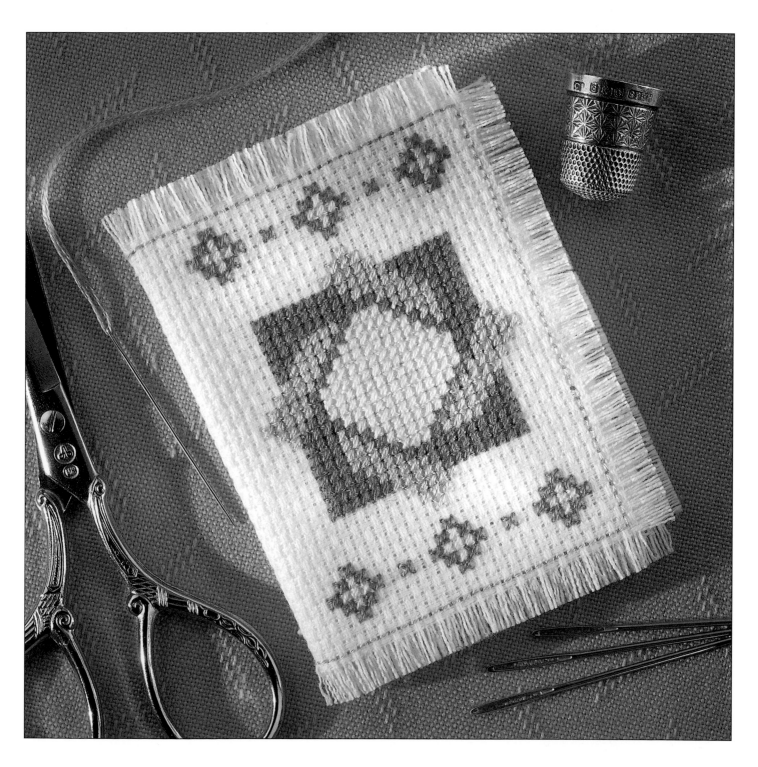

Pinwheel needlecase

YOU WILL NEED

- 3½ × 5¼in 14-count white aida fabric
- Madeira 6-stranded embroidery floss, one skein each of:

    Yellow 0112   0610 Pink
    Turquoise 1111   0911 Dark blue

- Tapestry needle
- 3¼ × 4¾in white flannelette for each double "page"
- White sewing thread
- Sharps needle

The chart shows the geometric design which decorates both sides of this needlecase. Each colored cross on the chart represents one cross-stitch worked over one block of the aida fabric, using two strands of floss.

To stitch the design, fold the aida fabric in half widthwise and work the embroidery on the front and back. Begin with the yellow diamond, add a pink outline, then work the four turquoise bands. Add the dark blue background square. Finish with the pink and yellow diamonds at the top and bottom.

FINISHING TOUCHES

To strengthen the edge before fraying the fabric, work a line of backstitch around all the edges using one strand of turquoise floss in the needle, one stitch above the stars at the top and two stitches below the stars at the bottom. Fray the edges to within a few threads of this line. Place the layer of flannelette in the center and secure it with backstitch.

FINISHING

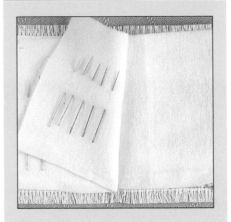

To add extra pages to hold more needles, simply stitch through all layers down the center of the needlecase to secure.

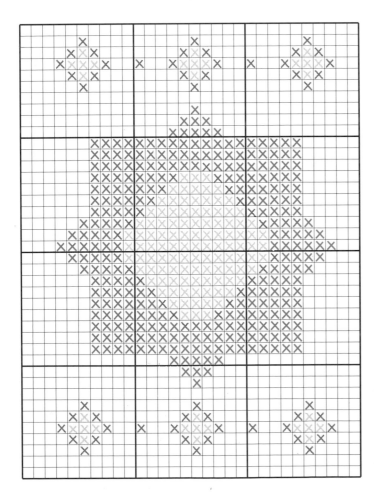

bright idea

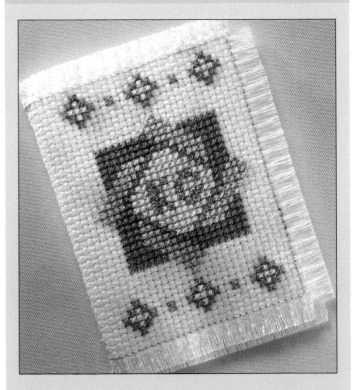

Personalize your needlecase by adding your initials. Chart them on graph paper before you start to make sure they are correctly positioned.

Breakfast linen set

Complement some patterned floral fabric with counted cross-stitch embroidery and quilting to make this cheerful breakfast set.

Breakfast linen set

YOU WILL NEED

- ⅝yd of 45in-wide patterned cotton fabric
- ⅝yd of 45in-wide white cotton lining fabric
- ½yd medium-weight batting
- 1yd of 2in-wide cream aida band
- ⅜yd of 22in-wide 28-count off-white linen
- 2¾yd of ½in-wide blue bias binding
- Madeira 6-stranded embroidery floss, one skein each of:

  Pink 0414   0801 Mauve
  Dark blue 0905   0906 Blue
  Light blue 0907   1113 Green

- **Off-white and blue sewing thread**
- **Tapestry needle**

cloth, and a napkin ring to match. The floral motifs used for the cross-stitch embroidery were inspired by the Art Nouveau period and have been worked in sympathetic colors to continue the theme.

CHOOSING FABRICS AND COLORS

The embroidery would suit any floral fabric in similar colors as long as the design is not too strong and overpowering. Alternatively, you could use a fabric with a completely different color scheme. In this case you will need to change the colors of stranded floss you use for the cross-stitch, trying to achieve the same balance of light and dark tones for the most successful result.

For a very fresh look, use fabric with a white, rather than cream, background and then use white aida band and linen on which to work the embroidery. Aida band is available in a very limited choice of colors, but it can be bought with a colored, decorative edging which you could match to one of the shades of embroidery floss.

When you are buying the floral fabric, try to avoid heavy or textured fabrics as these will spoil the finished effect of the design. Cotton lawn fabric is the ideal weight as it matches that of the aida band.

TRAY CLOTH

The embroidery on the tray cloth is worked on 28-count off-white linen (see page 72), which produces very fine results, and the edge is hemstitched (see page 113) by hand. It measures 12½ × 18½in.

Pretty bluebell motifs in pink, blue, and mauve complete each pattern repeat. The flowers and the leaves are outlined in backstitch using dark blue embroidery floss.

Take your piece of linen measuring 15¾ × 21¾in. Find the center of the left-hand short side and make a horizontal row of basting using contrasting sewing thread. Then measure 1½ inches in from the short side and make a vertical row of basting here. Measure another 1½ inches in along the horizontal center line and begin the embroidery here with the central flower of the floral spray, working in from the outer left-hand edge of the flower.

The color chart for the tray cloth border is shown on the opposite page, and the colors are given in the key. The chart shows one repeat of the pattern and one corner motif, and illustrates how to position the next pattern repeat after the corner. Each symbol equals one cross-stitch worked over two linen threads, using two strands of floss in the needle. The pink backstitch detail in the

---

This embroidered set includes all the useful items you will need to make a kitchen table or breakfast tray look pretty in the morning. It has a quilted tea cozy and placemat trimmed with an embroidered length of aida band, a finely worked linen tray

The picture below shows one complete pattern repeat. Green leaves and small bluebell motifs lead out from the central diamond.

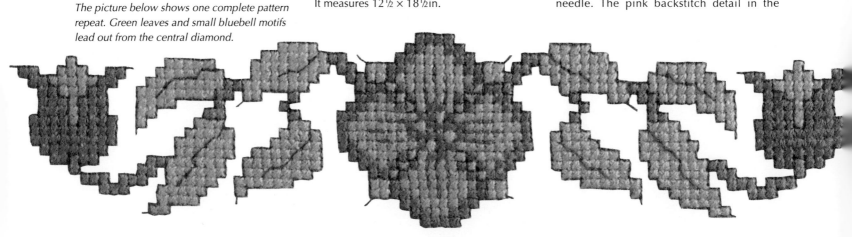

Corner motif for tray cloth   *One repeat of floral spray*

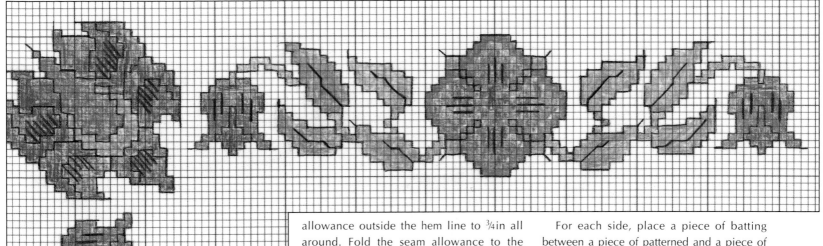

Follow this chart to work the floral cross-stitch design, turning the chart so that it is always facing the same way as your stitching.

KEY

Madeira 6-stranded embroidery floss, as used in the Breakfast linen set:

- Cross-stitch using pink 0414
- Cross-stitch using mauve 0801
- Cross-stitch using blue 0906
- Cross-stitch using light blue 0907
- Cross-stitch using green 1113
- Backstitch using pink 0414
- Backstitch using dark blue 0905

flowers also uses two strands of floss. The dark blue backstitching and details are worked in one strand of floss after the rest of the embroidery is complete.

Continue the floral border toward the corners and then work the corner flowers. On the long side, work two flower sprays with two linen threads between the complete sprays. Mark this center with a vertical line of basting. The center basted rows help you make sure that the other sides match exactly when you are working them. When the embroidery is complete, steam press on the wrong side over a towel.

Measure 1½in from each of the central flowers toward the outer edge of the linen. This is the foldline of the hem. Trim the seam

allowance outside the hem line to ¾in all around. Fold the seam allowance to the wrong side and press lightly. Miter each corner (see page 115) and turn under ⅜in at the raw edge. Pin and baste the hem in place. Work hemstitch around the edge with off-white cotton or linen thread, taking up four strands of the linen with each stitch (see page 113). Steam press the hem on the wrong side.

TEA COZY

The quilted tea cozy is trimmed with a length of aida band embroidered with the same floral sprays as the tray cloth. It is designed to fit a small teapot and is 11in wide by 6in high.

Cut a 20in length of aida band and find the center. Following the chart above, work three repeats of the flower spray, beginning centrally with the middle flower of the spray. Leave four aida squares between each repeat. Use two strands of floss to work the cross-stitch and the pink backstitch details. Then work the dark blue backstitch outlines and details with one strand in the needle. Steam press the work on the wrong side over a padded surface.

Using the tea-cozy pattern on page 91, cut out two side pieces in the patterned fabric, the lining fabric, and the batting. For the gusset, cut two bias strips of the plain lining fabric 3¼in wide by 20in long, joining pieces to make the correct length if necessary. Cut one piece of batting 3¼ × 20in.

This floral motif is only used when working the corners of the tray cloth. It is stitched using pink, mauve, green, and blue embroidery floss. The outline is worked in backstitch using dark blue, and it also has backstitch details in pink.

For each side, place a piece of batting between a piece of patterned and a piece of solid fabric, wrong sides facing the batting. Pin and baste together around the edges. Also baste extra horizontal and vertical rows to keep the work from puckering while quilting. Quilt through all layers with the blue cotton thread, following the pattern of the fabric with small running stitches (see page 111) or using the quilting foot on your sewing machine.

To make the gusset, place the batting between the two bias pieces and baste down each side. With right sides facing, machine-stitch the gusset to the two side pieces with a ⅝in seam allowance. Trim the seam allowances and overcast the raw edges with zigzag stitching. Turn the tea cozy right side out. Place the embroidered aida band along the gusset and pin in place, with the central flower at center top. With off-white sewing thread, stitch the band to the gusset with small running stitches along each side.

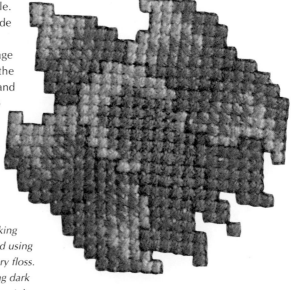

With raw edges together and right sides facing, machine-stitch or backstitch one edge of the blue bias binding around the lower edge of the tea cozy, joining the two ends neatly at the gusset seam. Fold the bias binding in half to the wrong side and slip-stitch in place.

QUILTED PLACEMAT

Like the tea cozy, the placemat has a lightly padded surface and is trimmed with an embroidered band and bias binding. It has a finished size of 12 × 18in.

Cut a 12½in strip of aida band. Find the center and work two repeats of the flower spray, following the chart on the previous page as for the tray cloth. Leave one aida square between the repeats. Steam press over a padded surface.

Cut one piece each of the patterned fabric, the solid lining, and the batting, each measuring 12½ × 18½in. Place the batting between the solid and patterned fabrics and pin and baste around the edge. Baste extra rows of stitches horizontally and vertically to hold the layers together while quilting.

Place the embroidered band on the mat where you wish, depending on your pattern. Pin and baste in place and work a row of small running stitches down each side of the band with off-white sewing thread, making sure the stitches go through all the layers. Quilt the rest of the placemat with small running stitches in blue sewing thread, following the pattern of the fabric. Finish the placemat

Use your quilting skills to make a lightly padded placemat to match the tea cozy. It has an aida band worked with the same floral pattern as the other items in the set and is bound with bright blue bias binding.

with blue bias binding around the outer edge, attaching it as for the tea cozy.

NAPKIN RING

The embroidered napkin ring adds the final touch to the breakfast set with a motif repeated from the main floral spray. Cut a 7in strip of aida band and find the center. Work the central flower of the spray at this point, with two leaves on each side of it. To make it into a ring, place the

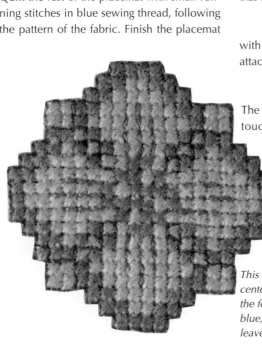

This diamond-shaped flower is worked in the center of each repeat of the pattern and forms the focal point of the design. It is worked in blue, pink, and mauve, and has small green leaves and stems on each side.

ends together with right sides facing and make a seam ¾in from the cut edges with off-white sewing thread. Finger-press the seam open, fold under the raw edges, and slipstitch in place. Turn right side out.

PRACTICAL

For very practical reasons it is essential that any fabrics you use to make the tea cozy and placemat are fully washable; this includes the lining fabric and the batting. if you are in any doubt, wash a small piece of your chosen fabric before you start. To see if it shrinks, measure the sample before and after.

POINT

Floral napkin rings

Create an elegant table setting with this pair
of cross-stitch napkin rings.

Floral napkin rings

YOU WILL NEED

- **3½ × 5½in 14-count cream aida fabric**

- **Madeira 6-stranded embroidery floss, one skein each of:**

  Light pink 0710   0705 Dark pink

  Light green 1501   1602 Dark green

  Yellow 0111   2208 Gold

- **Tapestry needle**

- **Cream sewing thread**

The floral design on these rings features intertwined gold and pink roses with green leaves. When the napkin rings are assembled, the flowers form a continuous garland.

STITCHING THE DESIGN

Before you begin, cut the piece of cream aida fabric in two lengthwise to make two strips, each measuring 1¾ × 5½in.

Follow the chart on the right to stitch the floral motifs. Each square represents one cross-stitch worked over one square of aida fabric. The solid line around the edge of the chart represents the total width and length of your finished design before you make it into a ring. There should be several spare squares of aida fabric around the design to turn under as a hem. The arrows on the edge of the chart mark the center lines.

Trim the excess aida fabric from each side of the embroidery to leave four complete aida squares. Turn two squares of aida fabric to the wrong side and use cream sewing thread and small slipstitches to secure the hems.

FINISHING THE RINGS

Once you have sewn the hems, use one strand of dark pink floss in your needle and backstitch along the sides of the napkin rings. Work this border one square out from the floral design and one square away from the folded edge of the hem.

Finally, make the napkin rings. Place right sides together and, with the cream sewing thread, use backstitch to join the rings into a circle. Work this seam through the holes in the aida fabric and along the edge of the stitched design. To finish the seam allowance, slipstitch it carefully to the wrong side.

To create a less formal-looking finish, you could fringe the napkin rings. Do not work a hem, but instead, tease out the aida threads that run horizontally along each side. Keep at least one full square unfringed to prevent the aida from fraying too much.

bright idea

If you wish to make napkin rings to match your china, experiment with different colors. The sample on the right shows the effect that can be achieved by using soft pastel shades of blue, coral, and green. A white fabric shows these colors at their best. To make each pair of napkin rings, you will need 3½ × 5½in aida fabric and six colors of stranded floss. Alternatively, you could use leftover skeins from your sewing basket.

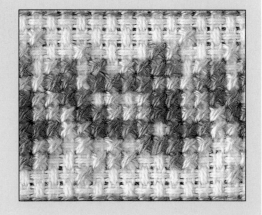

Jar lid cover

Featuring blackberries on the vine, a favorite wild fruit, this pretty cover will add country charm to your kitchen shelves.

Jar lid cover

YOU WILL NEED

- **8in square 27-count cream evenweave linen**
- **Madeira 6-stranded embroidery floss, one skein each of:**

  Dark green 1602   1609 Light green
  Dark purple 0714   0805 Purple
  Red-purple 0705   0503 Pale pink
  Deep pink 0708

- **Tapestry needle**
- **½yd of ⅛in-wide ribbon**
- **Cream sewing thread**
- **Sharps needle**

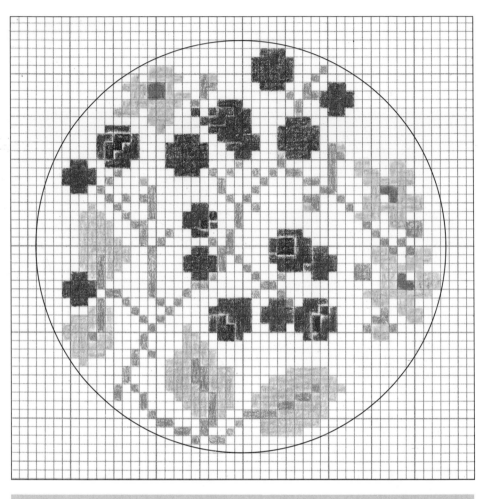

L ate summer is the season of home-grown fruits and homemade preserves. If you like to make your own preserves, what better way to present your wares than in a generous jar topped with a hand-stitched cloth cover?

The design features blackberries on the vine, showing leaves, flowers, and fruits in various stages of ripeness. The thread colors – luscious purples, soft greens, and pretty pale pink – are rich and subtle against the creamy color of the linen fabric. The finished circumference of the design is approximately 3½in.

If, until now, you have worked cross-stitch only on aida fabric, you will find working on linen slightly different. The holes are not as well-defined as they are on aida, but the threads still form a very even pattern. To work on linen, you count threads instead of holes. Work in two strands of floss throughout. Each cross-stitch is worked across two linen threads – follow the steps pictured here.

Before you start, prevent the edges from fraying as you work by sewing a narrow hem with small, neat stitches in cream thread, or trim the edge with lace or braid.

Secure the cover to the mason jar by tying ribbon firmly around it, and you are ready to put the jar in pride of place in your kitchen, wrap it up to give to a friend, or send it to a charity bazaar.

WORKING CROSS-STITCH ON LINEN

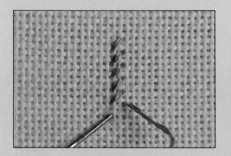 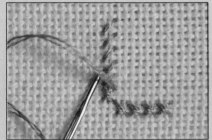

1 *As in most forms of cross-stitch, it is easiest to work in rows. Form a line of diagonal stitches first. To do this, work each stitch over two threads of linen, as in the example above. Start stitching in the center of your design and work out; find the center of the fabric by folding it twice.*

2 *When you have completed a line of diagonals in one direction, go back over the same line again, working diagonal stitches in the other direction, to form crosses. Stretch fabric in a hoop, if possible; it will be easier to work and makes the tension more even.*

Terracotta towels

*Thick terracotta bath towels decorated with geometric motifs
will look just right in a well-appointed bathroom.*

Terracotta towels

An ethnic border in rich, earthy colors adds something special to a pair of terracotta towels. The bold stylized design is simply worked in traditional cross-stitch along a length of cream aida ribbon and then sewn onto the border of the towel. The color scheme is influenced by the natural plant dyes used in ancient Aztec designs and is restricted to a few strong shades to give distinctive appeal. Although very few Mexican Indians today wear traditional costume, the women still embroider heavy cotton shirts, trousers, and belts using similar geometric designs to wear on special occasions.

Traditional cross-stitch is a neat, unfussy stitch that is ideal for use with a bold design.

For these terracotta towels, both the chart and the key to stitching are given below; on the key each colored symbol represents one stitch. The grid of the aida ribbon provides an ideal base for cross-stitch because it helps guide the stitches as you work the design.

Stitch with two strands of floss throughout, using a tapestry needle. To decorate the bath towel and hand towel shown here, measuring 30 and 22in wide respectively, you will need a 1½yd length of 14-count aida cross-stitch ribbon. This length will give you a ½in hem at each end. Repeat the pattern along the ribbon to the width of your towel. For a longer edging, aida ribbon can be bought by the yard from craft or needlework stores.

For the bath towel, start embroidering the repeat pattern at one end of the ribbon, first working a rectangular motif. Begin 2 inches in from the ribbon end to allow for the ½in hem, starting in the center of the rectangular motif and working out toward the edges. As you stitch, make sure that the strands of the thread lie smooth and flat and that the top diagonals all lie in the same direction: this will give you the even, neat finish that is

characteristic of cross-stitch. Once you have a particular color in your needle, make the best use of the thread by stitching nearby parts of the design which are worked in the same color.

STARTING AND FINISHING

Because the towels will have to withstand laundering, it is important that your stitches are secure, so start work with a long loose end, holding the thread behind the work; then, when you have finished working in that color, re-thread the needle with the loose end and thread it through a few stitches to secure it. Repeat this each time you begin a new

KEY

Madeira 6-stranded embroidery floss, as used on the Terracotta towel ribbon:

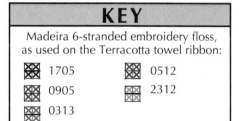

▨	1705	▨	0512
▨	0905	▨	2312
▨	0313		

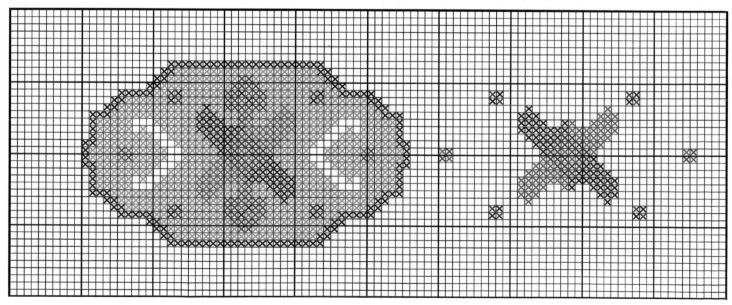

motif where there is no stitching into which to work your thread.

WORKING THE DESIGN

Work the outline, one arm of the cross, the two cross-stitches in the center of the blue flowers, and the two cross-stitches on the four top and bottom dots using forest green (1705). Next, work the center of the cross and the remaining two cross-stitches on the top and bottom dots using brick red (0512). Work the other arm of the cross, the remaining two cross-stitches forming the center of the blue flowers and the remaining two cross-stitches on the side dots in terracotta (0313).

Complete the rest of the detail by working the remaining two cross-stitches in the center of the cross, the flower shapes, and the remaining two cross-stitches on the side dots using azure blue (0905). Finally, fill in the background on the motif using sandy beige (2312), leaving the areas on each side of the cross blank to represent the cream shapes. Once the rectangular motif is complete, work the cross and dot motif in the same way, continuing to work the pattern in sequence along

The bold color mix of azure blue and rich earthy terracotta gives an ancient Aztec feel to this stylized cross-stitch border which incorporates a symmetrical motif based on the form of a cross.

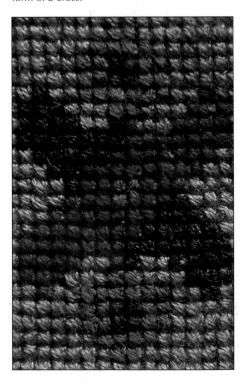

HOW TO ATTACH THE BORDER

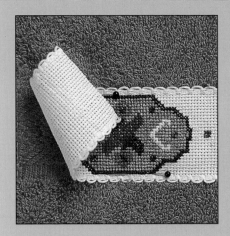

1 Center the ribbon along one end of the towel, making sure that the pattern is evenly placed along its width – leave an equal margin below and above the ribbon and ¹/₂in at each end to form a hem.

2 Make sure the ribbon is positioned evenly in the border strip of the towel. Pin the ribbon at regular intervals along the top and bottom edges, keeping it lying flat in a straight line along the towel band.

3 Once the ribbon has been pinned in place, turn the ribbon under ¹/₂in at one end to form a neat hem. Pin the end, tucking in the corners neatly. Repeat at the other end of the ribbon, making a ¹/₂in hem.

4 With the ribbon in exactly the right position, use a fine needle and cream sewing thread to secure the ribbon to the towel, using small, invisible hemming stitches. Lightly overcast the side edges.

the length of cross-stitch ribbon until you have completed five rectangular motifs and four cross and dot motifs.

HAND TOWEL

For the smaller-size towel, you should start embroidering the length of ribbon with the cross and dot motif – working the first dot 2 inches in from the end of the ribbon – and continue along the ribbon until you have completed a sequence consisting of four cross and dot motifs and three rectangular motifs.

This arrangement of the pattern will just fit the width of the smaller towel and allow room for side hems.

SEWING ON THE BORDER

Once you have completed all the stitching, you are ready to sew your ribbon to the towel following the steps shown above. Carefully center the ribbon along the band of the towel, leaving ¹/₂in at each end to make a hem; make sure the ribbon is positioned evenly in the border strip. Turn both ends under and pin in

When applied to soft and fluffy cream-colored towels, the traditional Aztec design takes on a feminine slant. When placed in a traditional, blue-painted bathroom with wooden accessories, the towels evoke the flavor of the Mediterranean. They would make a lovely personal gift.

place. Finally, baste the cross-stitch ribbon in place all the way around from the back before using cream-colored sewing thread and small invisible stitches to secure it firmly to the towel.

ATTRACTIVE ALTERNATIVES

The charm of basic cross-stitch lies in its simplicity and versatility. This bold ethnic design would look equally effective when applied across a wash bag, for example, which could be added to a matching hand or bath towel to make a special gift set.

The finished ribbon would also make a very attractive edging for a bathroom shelf. In this case, simply repeat the pattern as many times as you wish along the length of the cross-stitch ribbon, turning the edges under to form a neat hem. To attach the finished edging to the shelf, simply pin it in place with gold or colored thumbtacks or attach it with double-sided tape.

bright ideas

The stitched geometric border can be used to create distinctive curtain tiebacks. They can be stiffened with buckram and backed with a bias strip; the natural ethnic colors and simple motifs will bring a breath of Western climes into your home. Cut a bias strip of cream lining fabric and a strip of buckram, each 2in wide. Place the embroidered cross-stitch ribbon right side up on the buckram and baste along the length from the back, then back with the bias strip, placed wrong side to the buckram. Turn under the edges of the bias strip and sew in place using small, neat stitches and matching sewing thread. Fold and stitch raw ends under before attaching a curtain ring at each end.

Bird bell-pull

Embroider charming bird motifs on a traditional bell-pull to create an unusual wall hanging.

YOU WILL NEED

- **10 × 48in 11-count ivory aida fabric**
- **Paterna Persian yarns, one skein each of:**

  Red 841   824 Pink
  Yellow 711   652 Olive
  Dark green 660   734 Mustard
  Gray 463   421 Dark brown
  Rust 721   413 Toffee

- **Two skeins each of:**

  Green 611   623 Mint

- **10in cotton backing fabric, 48in wide**
- **Cardboard for backing**
- **Pair of 6in brass hangers**
- **Tapestry needle**

Wild birds, all native to the British Isles, are used to great effect on this charming bell-pull. Each of the five birds is perched in a different type of tree, and the whole leafy design is surrounded by a simple repeating border.

The design is worked on 11-count aida fabric using counted cross-stitch and one strand of Paterna Persian yarn. The chart is on pages 92–5. When you work cross-stitch with yarn, it completely covers the holes in the aida fabric and gives a denser quality to the colors and quite a different texture from that of stranded floss. Working in yarn also makes the bell-pull more substantial and therefore easier to finish.

With a finished size of 6 × 36in, it will grace

any living room wall or brighten up the fireside. The bell-pull is completed by backing it with a piece of stiff cardboard and a matching cotton fabric, and inserting purchased brass hangers. What could be easier?

PREPARING THE MATERIALS

Before you start stitching, it is advisable to bind or tape the edges of the aida fabric to prevent it from fraying as you work. Then to find the center, lightly fold the fabric vertically and horizontally. Keep the embroidery flat and taut by mounting the area you are working on in a small embroidery hoop. Always work with clean, dry hands.

As the design uses only one strand of the 3-stranded Persian yarn, you will find it easier to cut the yarn into manageable 15in lengths and separate the strands before you start work. When starting an area of color, leave a long end of yarn at the back and work your first few stitches over it while holding it in place with your finger. To finish off a thread, slip the needle under a few previously worked stitches on the back of the fabric.

KEY

Paterna Persian yarn, as used in the Bird bell-pull:

Ⓐ 841	Ⓔ 413	Ⓘ 623
Ⓑ 721	Ⓕ 421	Ⓙ 660
Ⓒ 824	Ⓖ 734	Ⓚ 611
Ⓓ 652	Ⓗ 463	Ⓛ 711

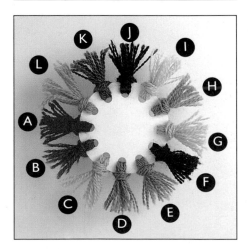

STITCHING DETAILS

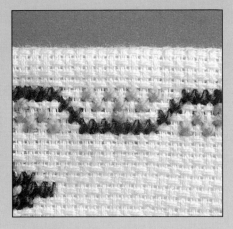

This bird's beak is stitched in dark brown and is formed by working one cross-stitch and two half cross-stitches to produce a slanted effect. The eye is one cross-stitch. The other details on the body are worked in various shades of brown and gold.

The plumage of the friendly robin is worked in mustard, toffee, and yellow, and his distinctive crimson breast in bright red. The beak and the eye are stitched in dark brown thread. Work a single half cross-stitch to make the pointed end of the beak.

The bell-pull border follows a wavy line of cross-stitch worked in green, one stitch wide all around. One stitch in red placed systematically here and there adds symmetry and balance to the border design. The rest of the border is filled in using pink.

When you have completed the design, snip off all loose ends of yarn close to the back of the fabric on the wrong side, as they might show through on the front when the bell-pull is finished.

STITCHING THE DESIGN

To stitch the bird design, work in counted cross-stitch using one strand of Paterna Persian yarn throughout. Follow the symbols on the chart on pages 93–95. Start at the center of the design by stitching the wren. Thread your needle with rust (721) and work around the wings and body in cross-stitch. Stitch the shading in mustard (734) and pink (824). Add the finishing touches to the wren using dark brown (421) to work the beak, eye, and legs. Use two half cross-stitches to form the slanted point of the beak.

Then stitch the leaves of the tree, starting with green (611) and then filling in the olive areas (652). Always finish one area of color before starting another. Add the dark green definition (660), the mint areas (623), and then fill in the branches using gray (463).

When the wren motif is complete, move on to work on the thrush in the apple tree. Start with the leaves using olive, counting the squares up from the top of the wren. Then fill in the shading on the leaves with the other green yarns. Follow the chart carefully when

choosing similar shades of yarn. Work the ripe apples in pink, yellow (711), and red (841) and the branches of the tree in dark brown.

The thrush is worked mainly in two shades of brown, rust and toffee (413), with mustard and dark brown spots added to represent the distinctive speckles on his chest. Stitch the beak in two cross-stitches and two half cross-stitches using dark brown.

When you have completed the thrush and the apple tree, embroider the great tit using yellow, dark brown, toffee, and gray. As with the other birds, the point of the beak is formed using a half cross-stitch. The leaves are worked in olive, mint, green, and dark green, and are surrounded by spots of toffee color for an autumnal effect.

SUBTLE SHADING

Now you can move down the bell-pull to work the robin redbreast in the willow tree. Stitch the bird itself using toffee, rust, and mustard for the shading. Work the breast in red. Then add the beak and legs using dark brown (see the Stitching Details, above). The leaves of the willow tree are worked in green and mint, and the branches are stitched in gray.

FINISHING THE BELL-PULL

  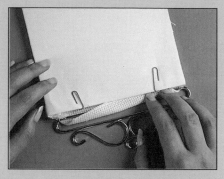

1 Trim aida to within 1in of the design and cut backing fabric to the same size. Place aida and backing fabric right sides together and pin. Baste and sew side and bottom seams in matching sewing thread, leaving 1/4in open at the bottom of each side seam.

2 Trim stitched seams all around and turn bell-pull right side out. Insert one of the brass hangers into the bottom of the bell-pull, threading the arms in through the spaces left open in the side seams. Overcast the front to the facing at each corner to secure.

3 Cut a piece of cardboard approximately 1/4in smaller than the bell-pull and ease it through the open (top) end. Use paper clips to hold it in place. Fold the fabric around the other brass hanger, turning the raw edges in. Baste in place and slipstitch the seam.

When you have stitched the robin, you can move on to work the oak leaves below in olive, green, and dark green. Then fill in the bird's plumage using rust, mustard, toffee, and yellow. Add the beak (see the Stitching Details on previous page for details), the eye and the branches of the tree using dark brown. The acorns on the tree are worked in toffee and rust with one stitch of dark brown to form the spot detail.

When you have finished all the birds and the leaves in the design, you can work the repeating border. Start in the middle of the lower edge, approximately 3/4in up from the bottom of the aida fabric.

Work the green line of the border first – doing this will give you points to refer to as the border design progresses. Then add the pink blocks and finally the red dots (see the Stitching Details on the previous page). Now that you have completed all the stitching, you are ready to assemble your bird bell-pull.

bright idea

If you do not want to work the whole bell-pull design, you could stitch the bird motifs separately and work as many of them as you like. The design has been charted so that the motifs can be stitched individually.

The bird motifs could be used to make a matching set of small cross-stitch pictures, with a common theme of the countryside and British wild birds. You could stitch all five pictures, or any number you wish, to decorate a kitchen or conservatory wall or to give to an Anglophile friend or relative as a highly individual and personal gift.

FINISHING TOUCHES

Finishing the bell-pull is very simple. First trim the stitched fabric to leave 1in free around the design. Then cut the backing fabric to match and, with right sides together, stitch down both sides to within 1/4in of the bottom seam. Stitch the bottom seam, clip the corners, and turn right side out. Insert the bottom hanger through the spaces left in the corners.

To strengthen the bell-pull, cut a piece of cardboard 1/4in smaller than the finished design and insert it through the open top edge. Put the remaining brass hanger into position, then turn under the raw edges and slipstitch the opening (see the steps above for details).

Now your bell-pull is finished and is ready to be hung in pride of place on your living room wall.

Baby's wall hanging

A commemorative picture with engaging motifs will bring cross-stitch charm to a baby's room.

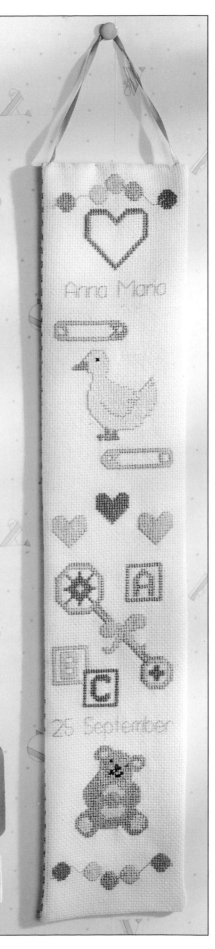

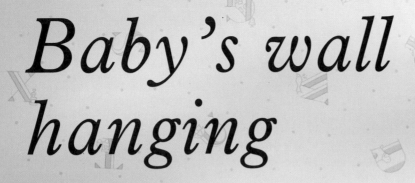

YOU WILL NEED

- **4 × 16in 18-count white aida fabric**
- **Madeira 6-stranded embroidery floss, one skein each of:**

Tan 2011	0109 Yellow
Cream 0111	0503 Pale pink
Blue 1012	0307 Peach
Coral 0214	1806 Light grey
Dark grey 1801	Black

- **Tapestry needle**
- **3 × 16in white backing fabric**
- **10in narrow ribbon**
- **3 × 15in thin cardboard**
- **White sewing thread**
- **Sharps needle**

Baby's wall hanging

ASSEMBLY DETAILS

1 *Place fabric pieces right sides together and pin. Sew around three sides in backstitch, eight squares in from the long edges and four squares up from the bottom edge, using sewing thread.*

2 *Remove all pins, trim corners and seams, and turn right side out. Gently push out bottom corners using scissor points and carefully insert cardboard stiffening through the top opening.*

3 *Fold top edges in. Insert ribbon ends through opening and pin to backing fabric, close to corners. Slipstitch opening, stitching through ribbon. Work two stitches of overcasting at corners to reinforce them.*

This cross-stitch wall hanging is a lovely way to greet a newborn baby. Childhood scenes in pretty colors are all part of creating an attractive environment for a baby, and this wall hanging is child's play to stitch and assemble.

STITCH THE DESIGN

Work the design in cross-stitch using two strands of floss throughout. Fold the aida fabric in half and then in half again to find the center point. Following the chart on pages 96–98, start at the center of the design and work your way outward to keep the design central on the fabric. Work cross-stitch in rows wherever possible for a neater finish and make sure that all the top diagonals of your crosses lie in the same direction. Try not to dot your stitches all over the fabric, but finish stitching

HOLBEIN STITCH

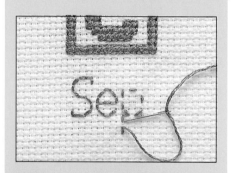

Holbein stitch is a straight stitch worked by stitching alternate lines of running stitch along the same line. First work a line of alternating running stitches across one intersection of the aida fabric so that the stitches and spaces are the same length as the crosses. Then work alternating running stitches along the same line again, filling in the spaces left between the first set of stitches (see also page 106).

each motif before you move on to the next.

Once you have embroidered all the motifs in cross-stitch, outline each one in Holbein stitch (see below) using a single strand of gray floss. Choose the letters and numbers you need to make up the baby's name and birth date from the charts on pages 96 and 125. Work the letters and numbers in Holbein stitch using one strand of gray floss.

FINISHING TOUCHES

When you have stitched the design, assemble the wall hanging following the steps illustrated at the far left of this page.

To give the wall hanging a softer look, you could leave off the backing fabric and the card stiffener and simply turn under the edges of the aida fabric and hem them in place with backstitch.

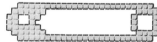

Whichever way you choose to finish the wall hanging, attach the ribbon as shown in the photograph and hang up the piece.

Make way for ducklings

Proud parent ducks head for the water with their fine brood of five ducklings
on this delightful border for a baby's quilt cover or crib sheet.

Duck family border

YOU WILL NEED

- **1yd length of 14-count white aida band, 5in wide**

- **Madeira 6-stranded embroidery floss, one skein each of:**

Pale yellow 0112	0108 Yellow
Golden yellow 0114	2006 Dark brown
Brown 2008	2009 Tan
Honey 2011	2203 Old gold
Gray green 1310	1602 Sage green
Olive green 1608	0913 Royal blue
Dark green 1404	1808 Gray
Aqua 1111	2101 Cream

- **Two skeins each of:**

Pale green 1409	1502 Green

- **Tapestry needle**

- **Striped yellow quilt cover or crib sheet, approximately 30in wide**

This charming cross-stitch border will be the focal point of a baby's crib set and will be treasured long after the baby has grown older. Five little ducklings proceed dutifully behind their parents in single file, probably on their way to the day's swimming lesson. The proud father leads the little procession; he has the typical colors of a mallard drake with his dark green head and blue and cream wing stripe. The female follows behind. Her coloring is more subdued, and she has subtle speckling on her chest. The ducklings are small balls of brown fluff with brownish-yellow feet. Behind the ducks grow bulrushes and other water plants, and the bright yellow irises add a splash of color.

The border is straightforward to work in cross-stitch on an aida band and would make a wonderful present for a new baby. When the baby has outgrown his or her crib, the border can be transformed into a wall panel which can set the scene for many a bedtime story. The finished border measures 30in long by 5in wide, making it a good length to trim most standard crib linen. Or it could be used

to trim a ready-made crib-sized quilt cover. If the baby is too young for a quilt, the border could be used to trim the top edge of a crib sheet or baby blanket. If you stitch the border upside-down on the wrong side of the top edge of a sheet, it will appear the right way up when this edge is folded over.

BEFORE YOU BEGIN

The color chart for the design is given below and on the following two pages. As it is so long, it has been divided into three sections, splitting just behind the father duck and between the second and third baby ducks. Each colored square equals one cross-stitch and the floss colors are shown in the key.

Before you begin stitching, find the vertical center of the aida band by folding it lightly in half and marking it with a line of basting stitches in a brightly colored thread. This will help you to begin stitching at the center and can be removed when the embroidery is complete. Overcast the raw edges at each end of the aida band to prevent them from fraying as you work. If you are using a piece of aida fabric rather than aida band, you will need to

bind the top and bottom edges as well to prevent them from fraying.

WORKING THE DUCKS BORDER

Using two strands of embroidery floss in the needle and following the chart below showing the center part of the design, begin stitching at the middle of both the aida fabric and the chart. When this section of the chart is complete, continue by following the left-hand side of the chart shown on the opposite page, and the right-hand section shown overleaf. As you start each section, check that the areas of stitching match correctly.

First stitch the water in aqua (1111) two squares up from the bottom of the aida band. To secure your thread when you start your first color, leave a short end at the back and work the first few stitches over it. To finish off neatly, slip the needle under the last few stitches at the back of the work and cut the end off. Work in blocks of color and do not pass long strands of thread across the back from one area to another as they may show at the front of the work. They can also get tangled in subsequent stitching and make the front look lumpy.

Continue by stitching the shading in the water with gray green (1310) and then add the grassy areas in various other shades of green. The two larger fern-like plants are worked in green (1502) and sage green (1602), while the small one is pale green (1409) and gray green. The iris on the left-hand side has pale green and sage green stem and leaves, and the flowers are in three shades of yellow. The tall bulrushes have stems and leaves in various shades of green; their heads are honey (2011) and tan (2009).

When all the foliage is complete, begin working the parent ducks. The mother duck has a tan head and chest with dark brown (2006) speckles. Her wing is brown (2008) with dark brown and honey feather markings. Stitch her feet and beak in old gold (2203) and lastly her eye in gray (1808).

The drake is more colorful. His underbody is gray, his chest dark brown, and his wing brown with honey feather markings and a dark brown band. He has a royal blue (0913) and cream (2101) wing stripe and a dark green (1404) head. The band around his neck is cream. His feet and beak are old gold and his eye is gray with a dark brown center. As finishing touches, outline the ducks' wings in dark brown backstitch and highlight their beaks and feet in tan backstitch, using one strand of floss. On the tips of the bulrushes, work a single straight stitch in green with one strand of floss.

THE BABY DUCKS

The little troupe of baby ducks is shown on the center and right-hand sections of the chart. Work the water and the grassy areas as

---

KEY

Madeira 6-stranded embroidery floss, as used in the Duck family border:

◐ Pale yellow 0112	⊡ Honey 2011	Dark green 1404
Yellow 0108	Old gold 2203	Gray 1808
Golden yellow 0114	Gray green 1310	Aqua 1111
Dark brown 2006	Sage green 1602	✛ Cream 2101
Brown 2008	✕ Olive green 1608	Pale green 1409
Tan 2009	Royal blue 0913	Green 1502

in previous parts of the design. The water plants are worked as for the ones you have already stitched, except that the dark part of the left-hand bulrush head is dark brown rather than tan. Add the five baby ducks in tan with brown wings. Some of them have speckles on their feathers in honey. Their beaks, legs, and feet are old gold, and their eyes are gray.

When all the cross-stitching on this half of the border is complete, work the outlining around the lower part of the ducklings' wings in dark brown backstitch, using one strand of floss. Emphasize the webs on their feet with tan straight stitches. Add single straight stitches to the bulrush.

ATTACHING THE BORDER

When the embroidery is finished, check the back to make sure there are no long thread ends which might work loose or show at the front and spoil the finished effect. Press the border on the wrong side over a lightly padded surface so as not to flatten the stitches. Turn under the raw edges at each end of the border and pin and baste it in position on the crib sheet or quilt cover. Sew the band on with backstitch, following a row of aida holes. If you wish, use stranded floss in a bright harmonizing color.

bright idea

There are a number of areas within this border which could be stitched on their own to create a charming picture for a child's room. If you wish to do this, choose a section from the chart and simply buy one skein of each color shown on that section. If small amounts of a color are needed, you may be able to use up leftover lengths from other projects.

Duck mini-picture

*Brighten up a wall with this friendly duck in his flamboyant
dotted bow tie – he will soon become a family favorite.*

Duck mini-picture

*T*oddlers will love this cheerful mini-picture. Find the center of the aida fabric by folding the square into quarters and mark it with basting.

Use two strands of floss throughout, except for the dark green outline and details. Start at the center and work the duck's body in yellow. Then fill in the gray bow with its red dots, and add the duck's head and beak and orange feet. Next, stitch the outline and wing detail in one strand of dark green, making one backstitch to each intersection of the fabric. Add the background crosses in two strands of blue, then frame your picture.

YOU WILL NEED

- 3½ × 3½in 18-count white aida fabric
- Madeira 6-stranded embroidery floss, one skein each of:

  Yellow 0744   0928 Green gray
  Red 0666   0740 Tangerine
  Turquoise 0996   0500 Dark green

- Tapestry needle
- 2½in diameter circle of cardboard for backing
- 2½in diameter blue frame
- Sharp scissors

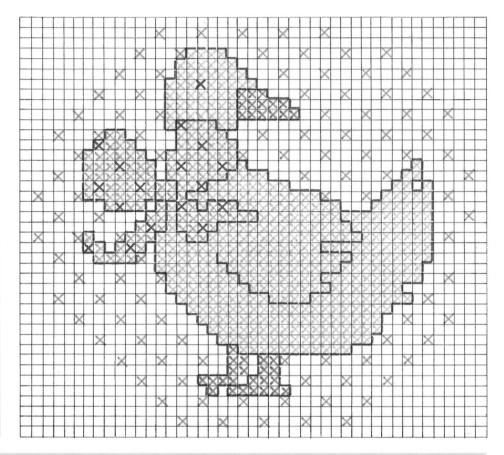

HOW TO FRAME THE MINI-PICTURE

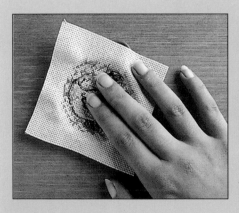

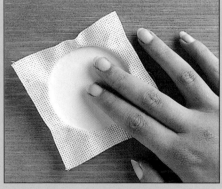

1 *Press the embroidered fabric lightly on the back with a warm iron, then position it in the frame face down. Make sure that the design is absolutely centered, with the hanging loop at the top. The blue background crosses of the design should just fit inside the frame.*

2 *Hold the stitched fabric in position in the frame while you carefully press in the cardboard backing. This card should fit firmly against the back of the fabric so there is no need to glue it in place, but if you feel it is necessary, seal the edges with a very small amount of fabric glue.*

3 *Use small, sharp embroidery scissors to trim away the excess fabric from around the sides of the frame. The tight fit of the backing card will prevent the embroidered fabric from fraying, so you can cut right up close to the edges of the card. Your mini-picture is now ready to hang on the wall.*

Clown bookmark

*Encourage a small child to read when you make this jolly
cross-stitch page marker.*

Clown bookmark

YOU WILL NEED

- 2¾ × 6in 14-count white aida fabric

- Madeira 6-stranded embroidery floss, one skein each of:

  Pale yellow 0112   0114 Bright yellow
  Orange 0207   0210 Red
  Blue 0913   1305 Green
  Black

- Tapestry needle

There is nothing more infuriating than closing a book or putting it down and losing your place; you have to flick through the pages to find where you stopped reading. Bookmarks were originally made from fabric or leather, and only in the last century have paper, plastic and other materials been used. The vivid colors of this jack-in-the-box will appeal to all ages.

HOW TO BEGIN

Mark the center of the fabric and follow the chart to work the design. Begin by working the backstitch edging around the entire design, using two strands of yellow (0112). This will give you a border to help you to place the clown centrally. However, do not fringe the edges until you have finished stitching the entire design because this will weaken the aida.

WORKING THE DESIGN

Begin by stitching the book cover in green (1305) and then work its spine using orange (0207). Next, work the base of the clown's bow tie in navy blue (0913), and don't forget the five stitches just above his bow. Fill in the bow and move on to his pointed hat, using yellow. Work his fluffy hair in gold (0114) and stitch the pompons on his hat and his facial features in red (see Stitching Details below).

Work the box with a red (0210) side and lid, a gold diamond, and navy blue inside. The two left-hand rows of the bow are worked in orange. Finish by working all the backstitching on the book cover and box and for the coiled spring in black (see the Stitching Details below). Remove the aida threads from the outer squares of your fabric to make a fringe.

As you are stitching the clown design, try to make sure that you finish off your thread ends neatly on the reverse side of your aida because they will show from behind when you have finished the bookmark. Cut the excess threads off, leaving only small ends to secure.

STITCHING DETAILS

The clown's eyes consist of four red cross-stitches around a single black one. His nose and mouth are also worked in red, and all the features are backstitched in black.

At the lower edge of the bookmark, the clown emerges from a box worked in red, orange, blue, and gold. The coiled spring is worked in black backstitch using just one strand.

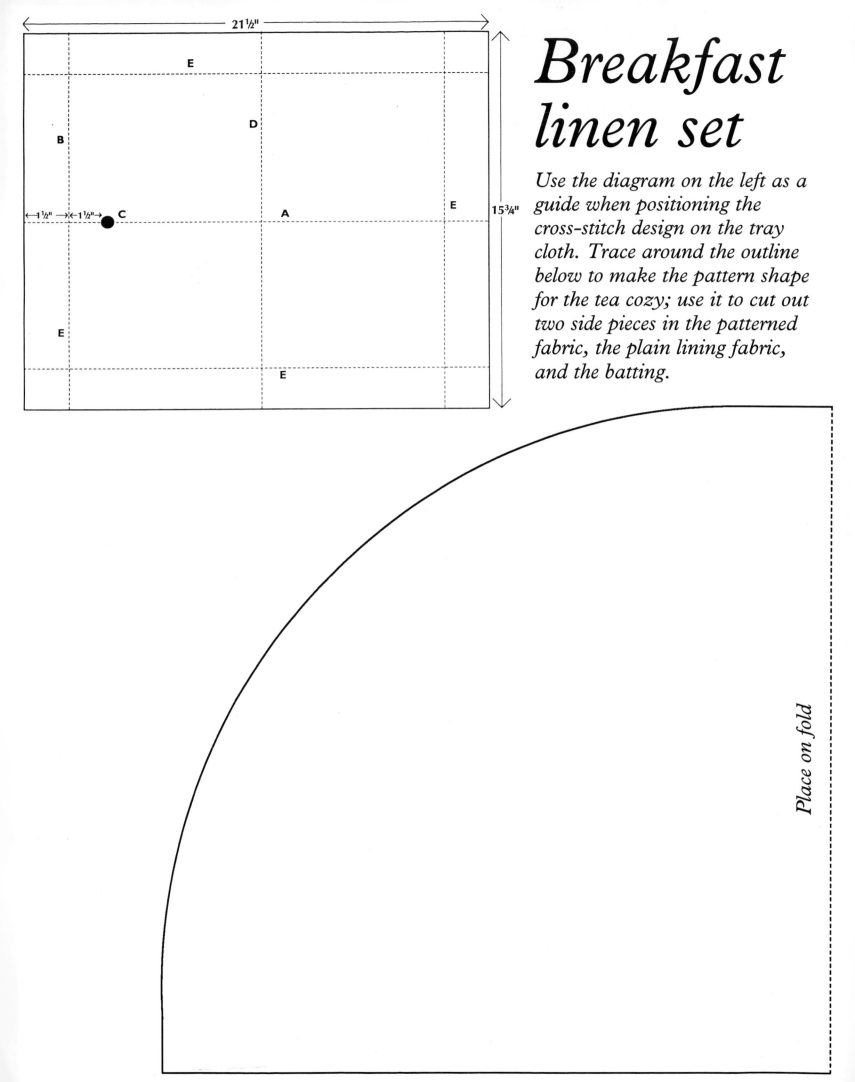

Breakfast linen set

Use the diagram on the left as a guide when positioning the cross-stitch design on the tray cloth. Trace around the outline below to make the pattern shape for the tea cozy; use it to cut out two side pieces in the patterned fabric, the plain lining fabric, and the batting.

21½"

15¾"

E

D

B

1½" 1½" C

E

E

A

E

E

Place on fold

Bird bell-pull

Use this chart and key (below and following pages) to work the cross-stitch design for the bell-pull. Each square on the chart represents one cross-stitch worked over one square of aida fabric. Take care when matching each section of the design on each side of the "overlap" line.

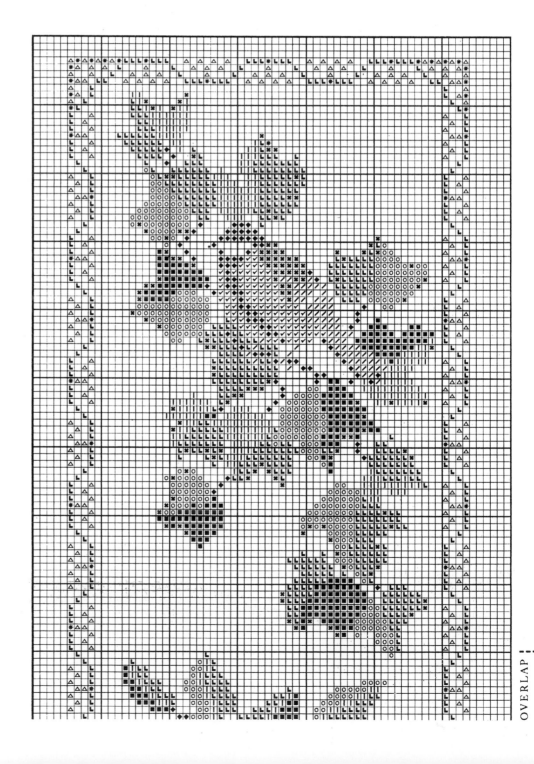

KEY

Paterna Persian yarn,
as used in the Bird bell-pull:

841		623		413	
711		463		652	
611		734		824	
660		421		721	

KEY

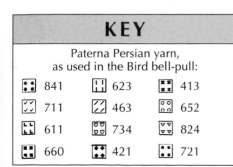

Paterna Persian yarn,
as used in the Bird bell-pull:

⬚	841	⬚	623	⬚	413
⬚	711	⬚	463	⬚	652
⬚	611	⬚	734	⬚	824
⬚	660	⬚	421	⬚	721

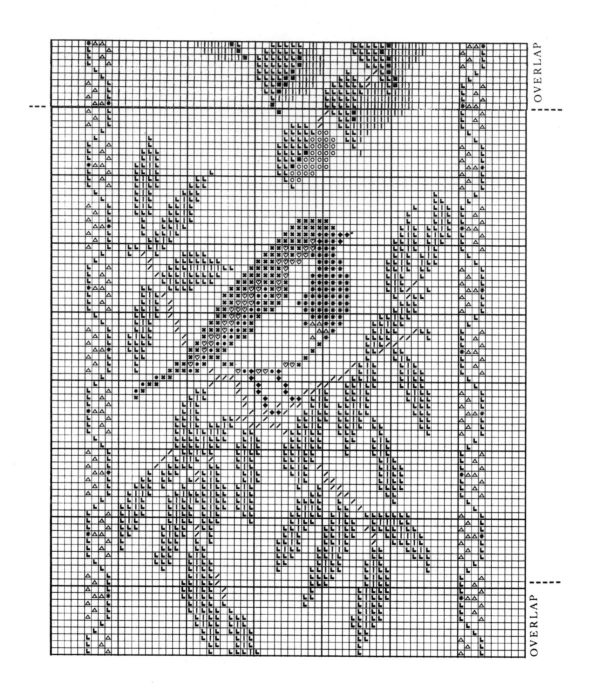

KEY

Paterna Persian yarn,
as used in the Bird bell-pull:

⠃	841	⊞	623	⠿	413
✓	711	⫽	463	⠒	652
⠄	611	♡	734	♡	824
⠿	660	◆	421	⠒	721

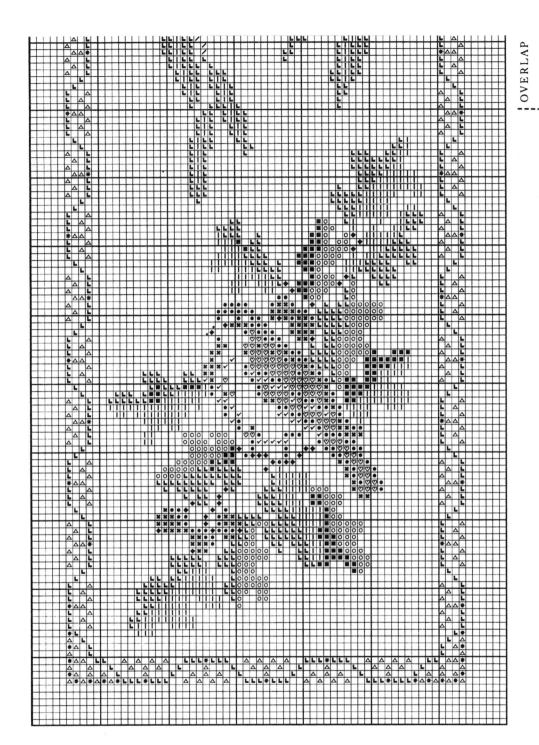

KEY

Paterna Persian yarn,
as used in the Bird bell-pull:

⊡	841	⊞	623	⊠	413
✓	711	⧄	463	⊙	652
⊔	611	♡	734	♡	824
⊡	660	⬧	421	⊡	721

Baby's wall hanging

Use this chart and key (right and following page) to work the cross-stitch design for the wall hanging. Each square on the chart represents one cross-stitch worked over one square of aida fabric. Make up your own messages using the letters and numbers on the chart below and stitch them in Holbein stitch. Take care when matching each section of the design on each side of the "overlap" line.

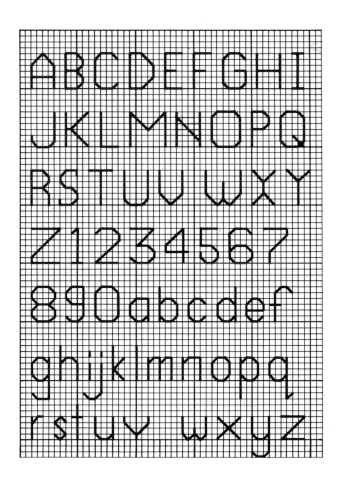

KEY FOR BABY'S WALL HANGING

A	Tan – 2011	N	Pink – 0503	T	Lt gray – 1806		
E	Yellow – 0109	O	Blue – 0102	■	Gray – 1801		
F	Cream – 0111	R	Peach – 0307				
M	Black	S	Coral – 0214				

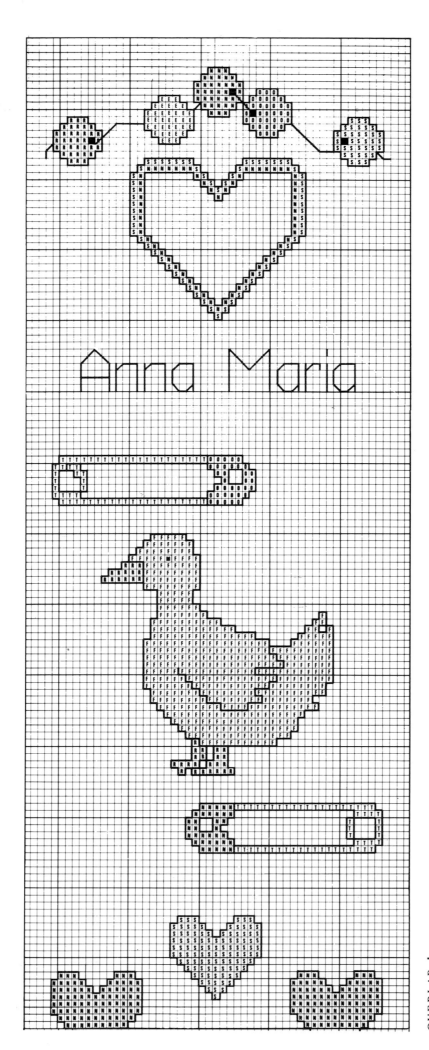

KEY

A	Tan – 2011
E	Yellow – 0109
F	Cream – 0111
M	Black
N	Pink – 0503
O	Blue – 0102
R	Peach – 0307
S	Coral – 0214
T	Lt gray – 1806
■	Gray – 1801

Anna Maria

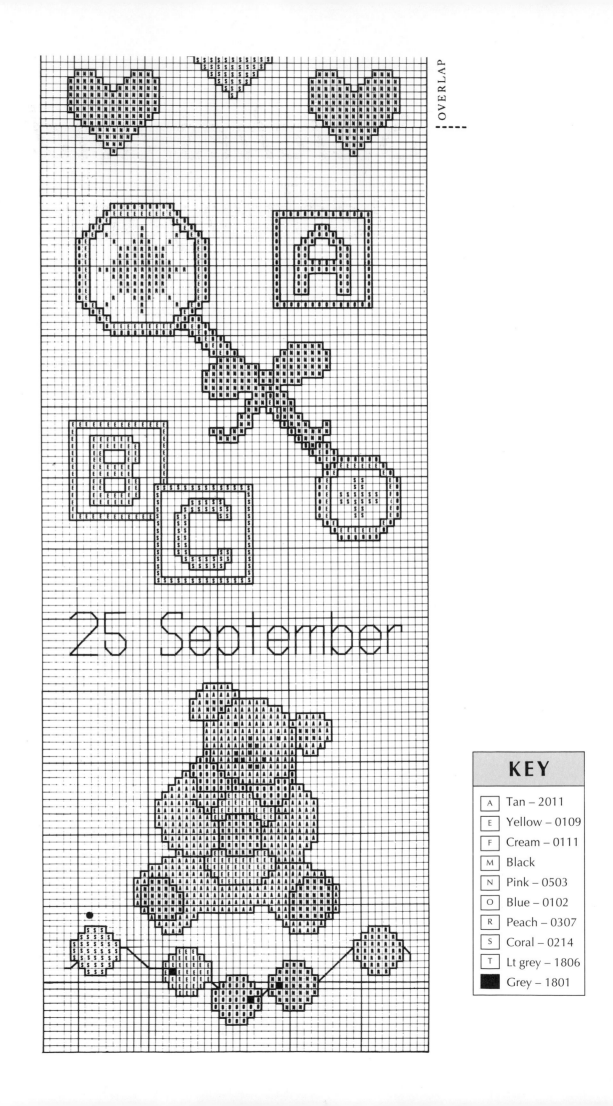

OVERLAP

25 September

KEY

A	Tan – 2011
E	Yellow – 0109
F	Cream – 0111
M	Black
N	Pink – 0503
O	Blue – 0102
R	Peach – 0307
S	Coral – 0214
T	Lt grey – 1806
■	Grey – 1801

Stitches and techniques

Introduction

*A*lthough cross-stitch is one of the simplest and most straightforward of all types of embroidery, there are a few basics with which beginners and addicts alike need to be familiar. The following section outlines the fundamentals of cross-stitch embroidery, as well as describing a few of the techniques that you might want to know about to help you complete the more intricate projects.

Both needles and threads, essential for any embroidery you might undertake, come in an array of sizes and types – and in the case of threads, a huge variety of colors – that can be confusing to the newcomer. We take you through this maze briefly, but you will probably find that you want to explore the field more thoroughly on your own by visiting needlecraft stores and exhibitions to see for yourself the incredible choice of threads and fabrics available.

Cross-stitch can be worked on any fabric, but is probably most effective on evenweave cloth, which gives each cross legs of the same length and size. Most of the projects in this collection are worked on aida cloth, the most popular of all the evenweaves available, but the selection is broad and worth exploring, as each type of fabric gives different results.

Some of the projects in *The Cross-stitch Collection* have been embellished with additional stitches. To guide those who may be unfamiliar with the English quilting or drawn-thread techniques used in the breakfast linen set, simple explanations have been provided in this section. French knots and straight stitch are other decorative stitches that have been used on featured items, and both are useful techniques to know. Straight stitch, the simplest stitch of all, is often added to cross-stitch

motifs to outline them, and can be worked to make beautiful borders.

The final section of this chapter provides a wealth of information about finishing your completed cross-stitch projects. The most beautifully embroidered piece can be ruined by a poor finish, but all the techniques here are simple to do and will give a professional look to all your work. Making your own pillow forms, tassels, and cords and braids is not only much less expensive than buying ready-made ones; it also means that your finished item will be "all of a piece," as you can use the same thread and fabric for finishing and match your colors exactly, and you can enjoy the satisfaction that goes with doing the whole job.

So don't worry about what to do with your completed embroidery – just follow the clear step-by-step instructions in each section, and you are on your way.

Needles

Needles are, of course, essential items of sewing equipment.
Stock your sewing box with a selection of different types,
and you'll always be sure of having just the right needle for each project.

For every stitching project, you need a needle – but what kind? There are so many different types and different sizes available that it's easy to become confused. Rest assured, however, that most of the rules for which needle you use for which type of embroidery are just common sense.

CHOOSING A NEEDLE

The size of your needle depends mainly on the size of your thread. The eye of the needle should be big enough to allow you to thread it easily, but small enough to hold the thread reasonably firmly once it is threaded. If the eye of your needle is too big, the thread will keep slipping out while you are sewing. The body of the needle should be just wide enough to draw the thread through your chosen fabric easily. If the needle is too fine, you will have to pull the thread through unnecessarily hard, which will affect the flow of your sewing and the tension of the stitches. If your needle is too large, you will make holes in the fabric that may not be hidden by the thread once it is pulled through.

The type of needle you use also depends on the kind of embroidery that you are doing. The two categories of needle are those with sharp tips and those with rounded or blunt tips. Sharp-tipped needles are used for most

kinds of surface embroidery on ordinary closely woven fabrics, and are available in several styles and many sizes to suit different threads and techniques.

Needles with rounded points, generally known as tapestry needles, are ideal for most cross-stitch. They are used for stitching on fabrics with noticeable holes, such as even-weave linen, aida fabric, binca cloth, and different types of canvas. Needles used on these fabrics do not need to pierce a hole to draw the thread through – in fact, a sharp tip is usually a drawback because it tends to split the threads and can spoil the look of the finished piece.

NEEDLE TYPES

Below are listed the most common types of needle you will come across when planning embroidery and craft projects.

Tapestry needles (A) have blunt tips; they are available in many sizes to suit every kind of evenweave fabric from fine linen to binca. These needles are the most suitable for use with aida fabric.

Crewels (B) are the most frequently used embroidery needles; they are available in many sizes and have a large, long eye that is ideal for threads such as stranded floss, pearl cotton, and soft matte thread.

Sharps (C) are fine needles with small eyes, useful for ordinary sewing thread, flower thread, and *coton à broder*. They are ideal for working hemming stitches and basting stitches on fine fabrics.

Betweens (D) are sharp needles which are slightly shorter than sharps and can be useful for fine quilting projects.

Quilting needles (E) come in many sizes; they are often long, so that you can take several stitches at one time with them.

Beading needles (F) are long and very fine so they will pass through the fine holes in small beads without breaking them.

Chenilles (G) are fairly large, sharp needles that have an extra-large eye to use with thick threads and yarns.

Rug needles (H) are like extra-large tapestry needles and are used for stitched rugs either on canvas or large-gauge binca.

Bodkins (I) are large, blunt needles which can be used for threading yarn and elastic through casings and ribbon through eyelets.

Blanket needles (J) are very strong semi-circular needles used in upholstery projects.

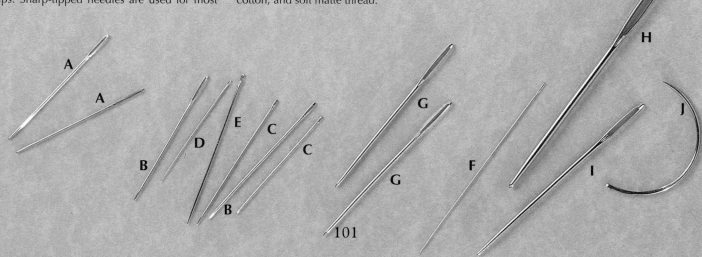

USING DIFFERENT NEEDLES

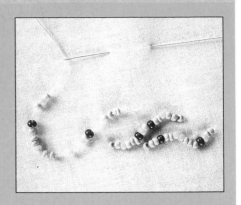

When you are embroidering in stranded floss or a similar thread on closely woven fabric, a **crewel needle** is usually the best needle to use.

For single threads which you are using for embroidery stitches or for couching down thicker threads, choose a fine **sharps**, **between,** or **crewel** needle.

Beading needles are especially long and fine so that they can pass through the tiny holes in small beads. For larger beads, use ordinary sharps and crewels.

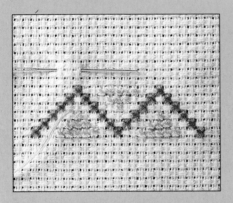

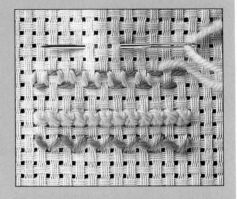

When you are working on fine evenweave fabric such as linen, hardanger or aida fabric, use a fine or medium **tapestry needle** that will not split the threads as you stitch.

Large-holed canvas or aida fabrics need to be worked with thicker threads and yarns to cover the background, so you will need a large-eyed **tapestry needle**.

If you are working on binca fabric or rug canvas which has very large holes, use a large tapestry needle or a special large-eyed **rug needle** which will be easy to thread.

WHAT WENT WRONG?

If the appearance of your embroidery does not seem quite right, you may discover that you have been using the wrong needle for the task.

In the first example, a crewel needle has been used instead of a blunt tapestry needle. The sharp tip has split the threads of the aida, producing uneven and unattractive cross-stitches.

In the second example, the needle is much too large for the background fabric and has a blunt tip instead of a sharp one. It has made large holes in the fabric, and the thread is too fine to fill and cover them.

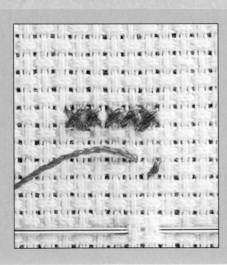

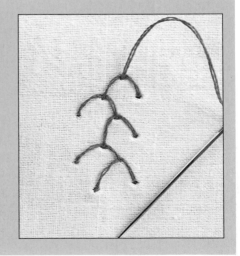

Threads

Any kind of thread can be used in embroidery, even ribbons, string, or strips of leather; but cotton, wool, and silk form the basis for nearly all classic stitching styles.

Clockwise from top right: fine silk in color-toned skeins, thick twisted silk, coton à broder, variegated cotton and pearl cotton; two wool yarns in stranded and twisted forms, matte embroidery cotton, and metallic threads.

Your choice of thread is affected by many factors, both practical and artistic. Some embroidery or needlepoint stitches require a particular thread or yarn, and you should always try to use a thread which can be worked easily on your ground fabric.

In general, threads can be divided into two types: stranded and twisted. Twisted threads are made up of plies, which cannot be pulled apart, but stranded threads can be easily separated and recombined to give the thickness of thread you need. A ply is a single thread of spun yarn and, generally, the more plies, the thicker the yarn. Each of the three strands of yarn that make up Persian yarn, for example, consists of two plies which cannot be separated.

COTTON

Different weights and types of cotton thread are suitable for surface embroidery and counted, drawn, and pulled-thread work. The strands of six-stranded embroidery floss are easily divided for fine work – or it can be used as it comes.

Soft embroidery cotton is a matte, medium-weight (5-ply), twisted thread, suitable for use on heavier fabrics, while pearl cotton (also called *perlé*) is somewhat finer. This 2-ply thread has a lustrous finish and is used in embroidery and also for smocking. It

is available in four different thicknesses: 3 (heavy), 5 (medium), 8 (fine), and 12 (very fine). *Coton à broder* is a twisted thread, finer than pearl cotton, but with similar uses.

WOOL

Crewel yarn is a 2-ply woolen yarn in which the single strand is slightly finer than one strand of Persian yarn. Unlike knitting yarns, crewel yarn does not fray easily when pulled through fabric, so it is used in embroidery on heavy ordinary and even-weave fabrics in crewel work, and several strands thick for needlepoint.

Persian yarn is made up of three 2-ply strands and is the best choice for needlepoint on canvas, because you can vary the thickness to suit the gauge of the canvas. The same is not true of tapestry yarn, a thick 4-ply wool, which is slightly finer than three strands of Persian yarn.

OTHER THREADS

Use silk thread for fine work on fine fabric. Available in stranded and twisted forms, it gives a lovely finish, and the results more than justify the higher cost. Similarly, linen is sold as matte thread for smocking and counted thread work, and in its shiny form for cutwork and drawn thread work. Synthetic metallic threads are available in various weights, textures, and colors. They are ideal for highlighting or for small areas of solid stitching.

DIFFERENT EFFECTS WITH THREADS

Embroidery cotton – sold as coton à broder – a twisted cotton available in different plies, suitable for delicate embroidery on fine fabrics. As it is so fine, it is unsuitable for work on canvas or looseweave fabrics.

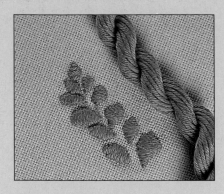

Matte embroidery cotton – a soft, 5-ply twisted thread, ideal for work on medium- to loose-weave fabrics. Its thickness gives it good covering properties, making it suitable for fine needlepoint work, too.

Pearl cotton – a thick, twisted 2-ply cotton, this shiny thread gives an attractive finish with a slight sheen. Suitable for use on medium- to loose-weave fabrics and on fine needlepoint canvas.

Variegated cotton – a 2-ply pearlized cotton, thinner than regular pearl cotton, with subtle repeating changes of shade down its length. The shading produces delicate effects in finished embroidery.

Crewel yarn – a twisted yarn that is suitable as a single strand for use on medium- to loose-weave fabrics, or for needlepoint on canvas in several thicknesses, depending on the gauge of the canvas.

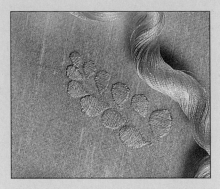

Silk – a fine, twisted 2-ply silk thread suitable for the finest embroidery on delicate fabrics. As it is so fine, it is sometimes easier to work with this silk using several thicknesses for better cover, as above.

Embroidery silk – this six-stranded thread can be used in any thickness to create satin-like effects. Although it is more expensive than cotton floss, the results are well worth the extra cost.

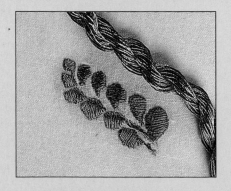

Metallic thread – available in various thicknesses and with different degrees of metallic content, these threads can be used alone or, in the case of very fine metallics, mixed with plain threads to give highlights.

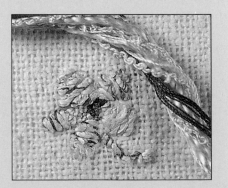

Mixed silks – sold in hanks consisting of a bouclé thread, a thick soft thread, and strands of fine plain and variegated silk in harmonizing colors, these blends are effective when used on loose weaves and knits.

Counted cross-stitch

Probably the oldest embroidery stitch of all, and certainly one of the quickest and easiest, counted cross-stitch is worked all over the world, in countries as far removed from each other as Mexico and India.

Cross-stitch has many uses. It can be worked as an outline or border, or as a filling stitch, and lends itself particularly well to lettering and motifs. Worked on canvas, it is very hard-wearing, so it is a good choice for upholstery.

Counted cross-stitch is usually stitched on special evenweave fabrics, such as aida, hardanger, linda or binca, or on canvas, because these make it easier to count threads, and the whole effect of the stitch depends on its regularity. Each cross-stitch should make a perfect square, being worked down and across over an equal number of threads.

Designs for counted cross-stitch are almost always presented in chart form, where one cross or symbol or block of color denotes a single stitch. Using these charts is easy — you literally count your way across the design.

There are several ways of working basic cross-stitch. Choose your method according to the fabric or canvas you will be working on. When working cross-stitch on canvas, or making only the odd cross-stitch here and there, it is best to complete each cross before moving on to the next one.

If you are working cross-stitch in rows on an evenweave material, first work a line of diagonals in one direction, then cover them with "top" diagonals worked in the opposite direction. By doing this, you get a more even tension and finish. A variation of this, called alternate cross-stitch, involves working every other diagonal from right to left, then filling in the gaps by working another row of diagonals in the same direction before working the top diagonals in the same way. This method gives an even more regular tension and so is a good choice if you want to fill a very large area with cross-stitch.

One rule applies to all methods: the top diagonal stitches must always lie in the same direction. If they do not, they will reflect the light differently from the other stitches and will stand out clearly as mistakes. The only exception is when you actually want to produce an uneven or irregular effect.

OUTLINE STITCH

Use Holbein stitch (also known as double running stitch) in combination with cross-stitch to outline and emphasize solidly stitched shapes and also to work decorative linear details. Holbein stitch worked as an outline is most successful when it is worked on an evenweave fabric so that fabric threads can be counted for perfect regularity.

Holbein stitch looks exactly the same on both sides of the fabric. It can be worked in straight lines or stepped to make a zigzag line when outlining a diagonal row of cross-stitches. The finished result looks rather like a row of backstitches, at least on the front. All the stitches should be of identical length.

Cross-stitch motifs can be as varied and colorful as you wish. From floral designs and alphabets to geometric borders, plain or fancy, you can create some lovely effects. Don't stick to printed charts either – try designing your very own motifs and borders. Take your inspirations from some of the stitched examples that appear here.

HOW TO WORK A SINGLE CROSS-STITCH

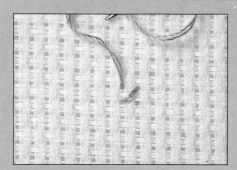

1 *Make a diagonal stitch to the lower left, take the needle through to the back of the fabric, and bring the needle back up at what will be the top left-hand corner of the cross.*

2 *Take the thread across the existing diagonal and insert the needle in the bottom right corner of the cross, counting fabric threads to make sure each cross is worked over a square.*

HOW TO WORK CROSS-STITCH IN ROWS

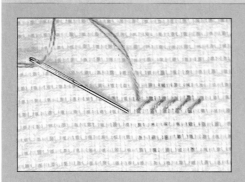

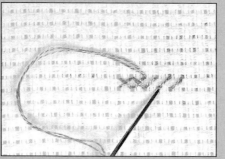

1 *Make a diagonal stitch from top right to lower left. Bring needle out through the hole next to the start of the first stitch, ready to form the next, and continue.*

2 *At the end of the row, change direction and complete the crosses by working another row, this time working each diagonal from upper left to lower right.*

Various evenweave cotton and linen fabrics are specially produced for use with counted cross-stitch. The best-known is an evenweave cotton called aida. Three of the samples below are worked on aida; the 22-count fabric is cotton hardanger. Each sample has a different "count," which has been worked on the front in cross-stitch. The count refers to the number of holes in the fabric (those large enough to pass a needle and thread through) per inch. The holes are all the same number of threads apart.

As shown below, the count of your background fabric affects the size of each cross-stitch, and thus the scale and size of your finished design, quite considerably.

HOW TO WORK HOLBEIN STITCH AS AN OUTLINE

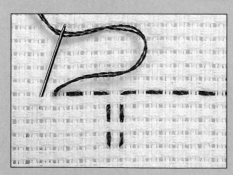

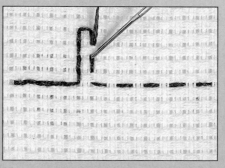

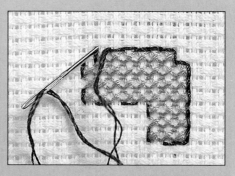

1 *Work running stitches from right to left, following the outline of the shape. Each stitch should cover the same number of threads, and the spaces in between should be the same size.*

2 *At the end of the row, turn work around and work back over the row just done, filling in the spaces with another row of running stitch. Keep the tension even at all times.*

3 *Outline a row of diagonal cross-stitch by alternately working horizontal and vertical running stitches. The Holbein stitch should outline the shape with a narrow, continuous line.*

Straight stitches

Simple to work and versatile, straight stitches are mainly used for working outlines and details. Variations of basic running stitch and backstitch can be used to decorate and enhance cross-stitch projects.

The basic straight stitches are running stitch, backstitch, and stem stitch. They are all easy to work and can be used in a variety of situations on both ordinary and evenweave fabrics. They all form lines – useful for outlining shapes, working geometric designs, and embroidering curved stems, as well as working intricate linear details. They can also be stitched in multiple rows to fill a shape; stem stitch is especially effective worked like this.

RUNNING STITCH

Although running stitch is the most basic of all embroidery stitches, it should not be ignored, as it can form exciting patterns when used imaginatively, and like many other simple stitches, it is often used as the basis of more elaborate techniques. Running stitch is also frequently used in quilting and appliqué. Double running stitch, generally known as Holbein stitch (see page 106), is worked twice over the same line, so that no spaces remain between the stitches. It makes a good outline, can be worked in one or two colors, and looks particularly effective on evenweave fabrics.

BACKSTITCH

Backstitch looks rather like Holbein stitch, but it produces a slightly raised line on the front of the fabric and is made up of longer overlapping stitches on the back. It has the appearance and something of the firmness of

machine stitching, so it is often used for closing seams when finishing articles such as throw pillows.

Running stitch, Holbein stitch, and backstitch can all be used alone, or they can form the foundation row for more complex stitches. In one of the most common variations, a second thread is woven in and out of the individual straight stitches to produce a whipped effect. When working a stitch like this, you will find it easier to use a blunt-pointed tapestry needle for the second thread. This will help you work the whipping row without picking up threads of the ground fabric.

All the stitches benefit from being worked perfectly regularly, unless your design actually requires a random effect. The weight of line each stitch produces can be varied by altering the size of individual stitches and by changing the weight and type of embroidery thread.

STEM STITCH

Stem stitch is a favorite choice for working stems, leaves, and tendrils in floral designs. You make this stitch by working a series of sloping, overlapping straight stitches along a guideline marked on the fabric. You can vary the effect produced by the simple method of changing the angle of each stitch worked, to produce a narrower or broader line. Stem stitch also makes an effective simple border around pictures, cards, and pillows worked in cross-stitch.

Practice the basic straight stitches together with some variations and create a beautiful border into the bargain by copying the border shown below. The stitches, from the outside in, are as follows: running stitch, double running (Holbein) stitch, whipped running stitch, backstitch, running stitch again, threaded backstitch, and stem stitch. The paisley motif in the corner includes stem stitch and threaded backstitch.

HOW TO WORK RUNNING STITCH

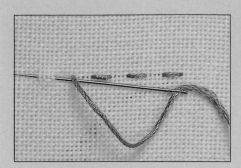

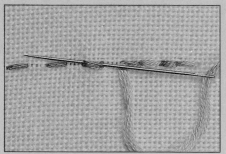

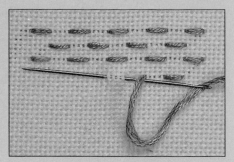

Simple running stitch is worked from right to left. Pass the needle through the fabric with an in-and-out movement. Keep the stitches the same length and the same distance apart.

To work **double running stitch**, also known as Holbein stitch, first sew a row of running stitches, then work a second row of running stitches to cover the spaces left on the first row.

Rows of **running stitch** make an effective border. Work a row of running stitches, then stagger the second row with stitches under the spaces in the row above. Repeat both rows.

HOW TO WORK BACKSTITCH

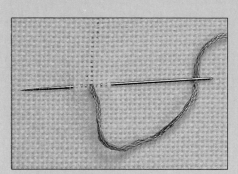

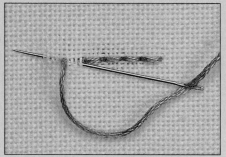

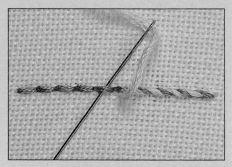

1 Pull thread through to fabric front and insert needle several fabric threads behind it. Bring point up same number of fabric threads in front of where sewing thread emerges.

2 Pull needle through in one motion, or make each stitch in two stages if fabric is stretched on a hoop. Repeat same sequence for each stitch. All stitches should be same length.

To work **whipped backstitch**, sew a row of backstitch, then cover with a row of whipping stitches as shown, taking the needle under each backstitch, not through the fabric.

HOW TO WORK STEM STITCH

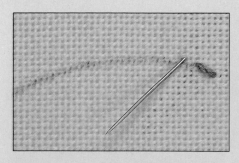

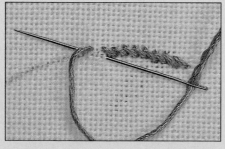

1 Stem stitch is similar to backstitch, except each stitch is at an angle to the guideline on the fabric. First, bring the thread through from the fabric back just above the guideline.

2 To make a stitch, insert the needle a little to the right, just below the guideline. Bring the point out to the left, just above the guideline, and pull the needle through in one motion.

To work **stem stitch as a filling,** work multiple rows, following the outline of the shape. Vary the position of the stitches on each row by making the first stitch slightly longer or shorter.

French knots

French knots and bullion knot are small, raised stitches which can be worked individually or in groups to add texture to surface embroidery.

French and bullion knots are very useful stitches as they add interest and texture which contrast well with areas of other kinds of embroidery such as cross-stitch. Both are worked individually, and they are often scattered at random across an area of fabric to make a light, textured filling for a shape. The stitches can also be packed close together to cover an area of fabric completely. Both French and bullion knots can be used as accent stitches, when they are worked on top of another stitch where a dash of color or texture is needed.

FRENCH KNOTS

French knots are also known as French dots and twisted knot stitch, and they are used on all types of fabric and canvas as accent stitches, lightly dotted on the fabric to make a powdering, worked close together to cover an area with texture, and stitched in rows to make an outline. French knots can also be worked over an area of canvas stitching to add texture or splashes of color. This is particularly effective when a silky thread is used for the knots to contrast with a closely stitched area worked in tapestry or Persian yarn.

French knots are quite tricky to work at first, and some practice will be needed before you can work them neatly every time. Work this stitch on fabric stretched in an embroidery hoop or frame for best results, and choose a fabric with a fairly open weave for your first attempts. Select your needle with care as you need to choose one with an eye large enough to accommodate your thread, but not so large that it is difficult to pull the twists through. You should use tapestry needles on evenweave fabrics.

You can use any type of embroidery thread when working French knots, but the weight of your chosen thread will determine the size of the finished knot. Begin by using a twisted thread such as pearl cotton or matte cotton,

which will be much easier to handle than stranded floss. When you have become familiar with the stitch, try contrasting three or four lightweight threads used in the needle at the same time, or mix two strands of Persian or crewel yarn with one strand of metallic blending filament. You will be able to achieve some interesting effects when the knots are massed together, especially if you substitute different threads at intervals when you are filling a shape.

BULLION KNOT

Bullion knot, also known as caterpillar stitch, produces a much larger, heavier knot than a French knot. A long, coiled knot is made which can be used in the same way as a French knot – as an accent, as an open or solid filling, or worked end to end in a row to make a heavy outline. The knots can also be arranged to fill a circular shape, beginning at the center and working outward. The result resembles a rose, and a group of bullion stitches arranged in this way is known as a Puerto Rico rose.

Bullion knots are rather difficult to work neatly, especially the tricky process of pulling the needle through the coil of thread, and it is best to work on fabric stretched in an embroidery hoop or frame so that you have both hands free. Use a thick needle with a fairly flat eye so that it will pass easily through the coil, and begin practicing with a soft, twisted

thread such as tapestry yarn on a fairly loosely woven fabric. As with French knots, the weight of your thread will determine the size of the knot.

Although traditional bullion knot lies flat along the surface of the fabric, you can work an interesting variation that creates a three-dimensional surface. To do this, wrap the thread many more times around the needle when making each knot. The coil of thread will then be too long to lie flat on the fabric and will make a small hump instead. By working the stitch in a heavyweight wool thread and arranging the knots close together, you can produce a highly textured effect.

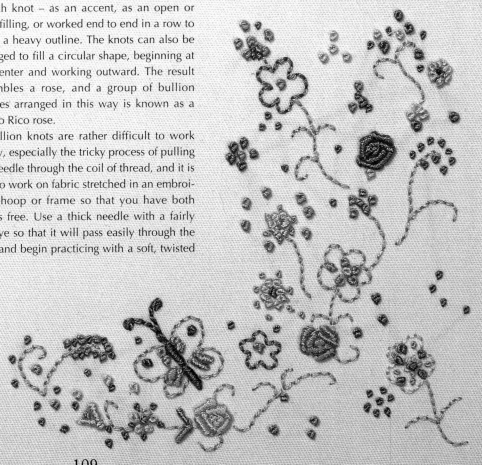

HOW TO WORK A FRENCH KNOT

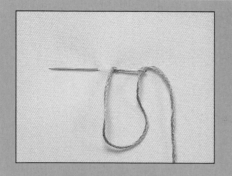

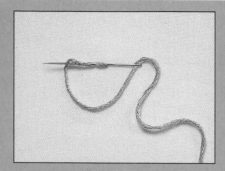

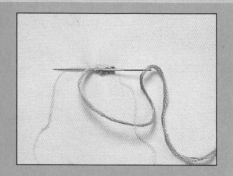

1 Hold point of needle close to point where thread emerges and, holding the thread taut with the left hand, wind thread around the needle two or three times.

2 Holding thread in the left hand, tighten the twists and insert the needle in the fabric a few threads from where it emerged. Pull through to back of fabric to secure knot.

3 To fill a shape, begin at top right-hand edge, working knots in parallel rows. For a random effect, alter thickness of thread after every 10 or 20 knots have been made.

HOW TO WORK A BULLION KNOT

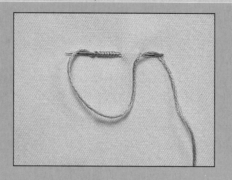

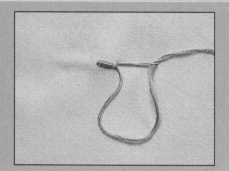

1 Bring needle and thread through to front of fabric, then insert needle a short distance from where thread emerges, bringing it out at same place as the thread.

2 Coil thread around point of needle six or seven times, hold coil down on fabric securely with your left thumb, then pull needle gently through the coil.

3 Pull working thread in opposite direction to make coil lie flat, then insert needle in same place as before. The coil should lie neatly on the surface of the fabric.

WHAT WENT WRONG?

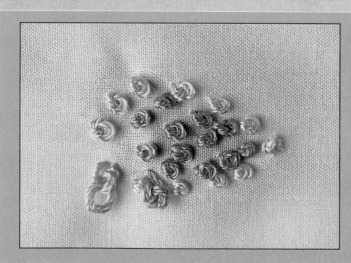

French knots can look messy if they are not worked correctly, as they will not sit neatly on the surface of the fabric. To prevent your French knots from working loose after being stitched, make sure that you hold the embroidery thread tightly in your left hand (or your right hand if you are left-handed) when you are winding it around the point of the needle; otherwise, the stitches could come undone.

If your French knots seems secure, but the thread is looking slightly looped, you might be twisting the thread around the point of the needle too many times before pulling the thread through the fabric to make the stitch.

It is a good idea to practice working French knots on a scrap of fabric before starting a new embroidery project. Don't despair – practice makes perfect!

English quilting

English, or padded, quilting is the traditional method of stitching textured patterns on padded fabric. It lends itself to all kinds of wonderful designs, both traditional and contemporary.

English, or padded, quilting is a method of producing a textured surface by stitching onto a fabric that has been backed by a layer of soft batting. As the design is stitched, it pulls the layers together and gives the work its characteristic molded texture.

In spite of its name, English quilting has a long tradition in other countries as well, especially in Wales and North America; it is also the main method of quilting designs on the plain areas of patchwork patterns. In England, spectacular quilts were stitched in the northern counties, and the favorite combination of white thread on a white background is still used to great effect in both traditional and modern designs. When a single piece of background fabric is used, the final quilt is known as a wholecloth quilt. English quilting was often used, too, on strip-pieced quilts, made from long strips of solid-colored fabric, and is still used on quilts produced to traditional Amish patterns.

QUILT DESIGNS

The designs for English quilting range from the very simple to the very elaborate. Each region where padded quilting was done developed its own favorite designs. These were probably passed around each area by itinerant quiltmakers who traveled from house to house or from village to village to mark the designs for housewives or quilt clubs to stitch. Many of the traditional designs are based on such everyday items as feathers, goose wings, flowers, leaves, and wreaths, and some of the most popular shapes were produced by drawing around easily obtained items such as flat-irons or the bottoms of buckets.

English quilting is an easy technique that produces very effective results even for a beginner. Most designs are worked in running stitch (although some quilters add chain stitch or stem stitch for emphasis), and the keys to success are to keep the stitches even and regular and to make sure that each stitch passes through all three layers of top fabric, batting, and backing fabric. It is best to take several stitches on the needle before pulling the thread through, as this leads to a more even stitching rhythm.

The best top fabric to use for this type of work is 100% cotton, as it produces a good finish and texture. For the quilting stitches, ideally use quilting thread, which is stronger than ordinary thread. If you cannot obtain quilting thread, use cotton sewing thread; polyester thread tangles too easily. Batting is available in several thicknesses and materials. For your first projects, use 2oz or 4oz-weight synthetic batting, which is easy to work with and fully washable.

This traditional feather design has a double quilted outline and is set off by a simple checkerboard texture in one corner. A soft pastel-colored fabric has been used instead of the more traditional white to give the design a more modern look.

HOW TO WORK ENGLISH QUILTING

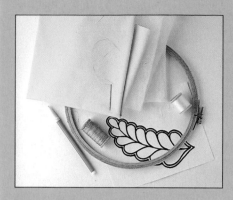

1 *For a simple piece of English quilting, you will need a top fabric, batting, and backing fabric, quilting thread and a long needle, basting thread, a frame, and some method of marking your design on the fabric.*

2 *Transfer your design to the front of your top fabric. Fabric marking pens are good for this, as the marks are very clear but are not permanent. Alternatively, use a sharp, hard pencil and mark lightly.*

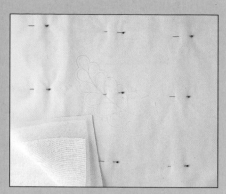

3 *Cut a piece of batting and a piece of backing fabric, such as cheesecloth, the same size as your top fabric. Put the batting between the cheesecloth and the top fabric, smooth them out, and pin the layers together.*

4 *Using basting thread and a long needle, stitch lines of basting horizontally and vertically across the area to be quilted. This holds the layers firmly in place while they are being quilted.*

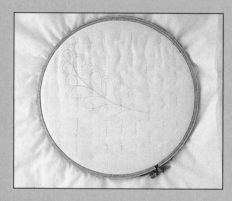

5 *Put the fabric in an embroidery hoop or a quilting hoop to hold it taut and prevent distortion while you are stitching. If you need to move the hoop around the fabric, take care not to damage any stitching.*

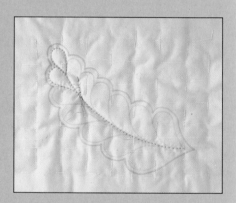

6 *Thread your needle with quilting thread and tie a knot in the end. Pull the needle through from the back and, beginning at the center of the design, stitch along the marked lines with short, even running stitches.*

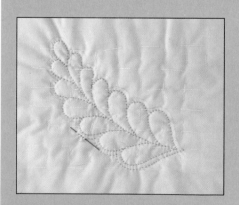

7 *Stitch your way from the center of the design to the outside edges. Working from the center outward in this way helps to prevent the fabric from puckering.*

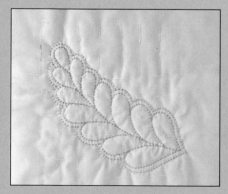

8 *Do not remove basting stitches until quilting is complete and then carefully unpick them using a tapestry needle. Take care not to catch any of the quilting stitches.*

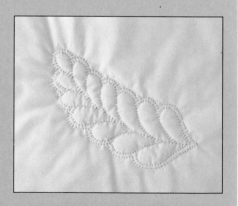

9 *If you have used a water-soluble pen, spray the quilted design gently with cold water. Pencil marks will fade over time (but may not disappear completely).*

Drawn thread work

Create beautiful borders with drawn thread work, a form of counted thread embroidery in which horizontal threads are removed and the remaining vertical threads are stitched together to form pretty openwork patterns.

This fascinating technique was used to decorate cloth several thousand years ago in ancient Egypt and has been used, on and off, ever since. Today, drawn thread work is most frequently used for working decorative hems on handkerchiefs, napkins, tablecloths, and bed linen. The same techniques are also used to make beautiful borders for collars, cuffs, and hems on clothing, especially blouses, skirts, and dresses.

HEMSTITCHING

The simplest form of drawn thread work is basic hemstitch, in which the outer edge of the border can also form the inner edge of a hem. Stitches are worked alternately to secure the hem and group the vertical threads in the border into clusters. The stitch, also called antique hemstitch, is worked on the wrong side of the fabric, and only the loops of sewing thread drawing clusters of vertical threads together are visible on the right side of the fabric. Hemstitch can also be worked independently of a hem, as a purely decorative stitch along a border of vertical threads. There are many variations on basic hemstitch, all of which are very attractive and some of which are quite ornate. The vertical threads in the border can be stitched, twisted, or knotted together in many different ways.

FABRICS AND SEWING THREADS

The best type of fabric to choose for drawn thread work is an evenweave fabric with equal vertical and horizontal thread counts and individual threads large enough to count and, more importantly, pull out. The looser the weave, the more open-looking the finished work will appear.

Evenweave linen is the traditional choice for drawn thread work. It is available with thread counts which vary from fine to coarse and heavy. However, there are many other suitable evenweave fabrics, including some synthetics which do not need ironing.

Choose thread which suits the thickness of the fabric. Cottons are best, including stranded floss, *coton à broder*, and pearl cotton. For coarse fabrics such as heavy linen, three or four strands of stranded floss or a similar weight of thread is suitable. For lighter fabrics, such as organdy or lawn, one or two strands of stranded floss would be sufficient. Match the color of the thread to the fabric for a subtle, traditional look, or use thread in a contrasting color for a more eye-catching effect. Always use a tapestry needle – the blunt point separates the threads of the fabric, whereas a regular sewing needle might split them.

WITHDRAWING THREADS

First plan where the border will be on the fabric and work out its exact depth. Leave at least half an inch of fabric between the edge of the border and the fabric edge. Mark the positions of the upper and lower edges with lines of basting stitches.

Then, using the blunt point of a tapestry needle, lift the horizontal thread immediately above the lower line of basting, halfway along its length, and carefully cut it with a pair of sharp-pointed embroidery scissors. Still using the needle, carefully unpick this thread, working from the center toward the ends of the border. Do not pull out, or "withdraw," the entire thread. When you come to the edge of the borders, pick up each half of the fabric thread in turn in a needle and secure it by stitching it back into the fabric beyond the border edge. Next, pull out the horizontal thread above the one you have just withdrawn in the same way. Continue to pull out threads of fabric very carefully until the border is the desired depth. As a general rule, the more complicated the border, the greater the number of horizontal threads you will need to remove.

The tray cloth border below is worked in basic hemstitch and diamond hemstitch, one of the simpler hemstitch variations.

HOW TO WORK HEMSTITCH WITH A HEM

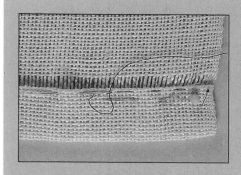

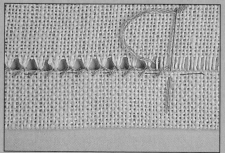

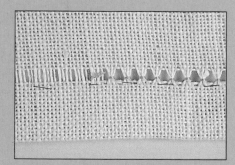

1 *(Back of work)* Calculate position of border by doubling hem length and adding ¼in for turning. Pull out three horizontal threads above this point, turn hem up, and baste in place.

2 *(Back of work)* Begin with a knot. Take thread behind four vertical fabric threads, from right to left, then across front of vertical threads; then stitch through hem allowance.

3 The border on the right side of the fabric consists of groups of four vertical fabric threads drawn together with loops of stitching thread. Finish with a knot under fold of hem.

HOW TO WORK HEMSTITCH WITHOUT A HEM

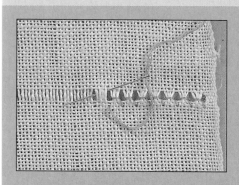

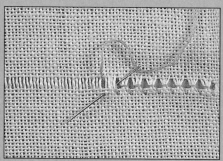

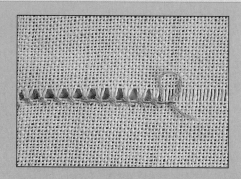

1 Secure thread to left of border with back-stitches, leaving a long thread. Working on right side of fabric, take thread under four vertical fabric threads, from right to left.

2 Pull thread through and take it over vertical fabric threads from left to right, then pass needle behind vertical threads again and bring it out below two horizontal threads.

3 *(Back of work)* To finish off thread end, run needle through several completed stitches, then snip off thread. Unpick backstitches at beginning of work and finish end in same way.

HOW TO WORK DIAMOND HEMSTITCH

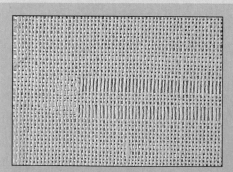

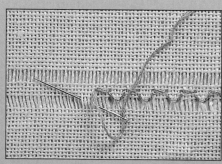

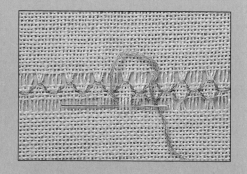

1 *(Back of work)* Pull out 3 horizontal threads, leave 4, then pull out 3 more. Finish ends by picking each one up in a needle and weaving it back through fabric threads.

2 Work a backstitch across 4 threads, take needle behind 4 vertical threads, loop thread over and behind vertical threads, and make diagonal stitch across 2 horizontal threads.

3 Turn fabric around and work second row in same way, again from right to left, stitching over backstitches running through center of border to create mirror image of first row.

Mitering corners

Carefully mitered corners add a professional-looking finish to embroidered items. Try these easy methods for perfect results every time.

There are several ways of finishing off the corners of an embroidered project neatly, but one of the most attractive and least conspicuous methods is by mitering the corners. Mitering involves stitching angled seams in the fold allowed for the hem. These seams are worked at a 45° angle to the corner edges of the finished item and give a very neat finish.

USES FOR MITERED CORNERS

Depending on your exact method of finishing, miters can be worked so that they appear on the wrong side or the right side of the work. Miters on the wrong side will obviously not show so much and are excellent for pieces of decorative household linen, such as tray cloths, table mats, and tablecloths, when you want a neat and hard-wearing hem with precise corners. One of the main benefits of mitering is that it reduces the bulk at the corners of the embroidered item, so the corners are flatter than if you finish them by simply folding them over square.

For other types of embroidery, you may prefer to work the miters so that they appear on the right side of your work. This method is useful if you want to catch down a hem with a decorative stitch such as herringbone, so that it becomes a feature of the design. You can also cover the raw fabric edges with a decorative strip, such as bias binding, lace, or eyelet lace. This technique works particularly well if you are working with a bulky fabric or a loosely woven one that frays or distorts easily, as you only have to turn over one thickness of the fabric for the hem.

MITERING METHODS

Although mitering gives professional-looking results, it is very easy to achieve; there is no mystique to it, just careful technique. The most important thing to watch is the first pressing under of the diagonal fold; you must be very careful not to pull or stretch the fabric

at this stage; if it is distorted, the miter will not lie quite flat. Evenweave fabrics are sometimes very loosely woven and easily distorted; you may find it useful to give the flat corners a quick press with spray-on starch before you begin the folding. This will give the corners a temporary stability while you work on them and also help to prevent the edges from fraying.

You also need to make sure that the fold is at exactly 45° to the edges of the stitched item. On evenweave fabrics this is easy to do as you can line up the raw edges of the folded corner with the warp and weft threads of the fabric. With other fabrics, you may find it useful just to hold the fold against a protractor before you press it, to make sure that the

angle is accurate. Once all the corners of the embroidery have been mitered, the hem can be stitched as usual.

The photographs below show the back and the front view of a neatly mitered corner.

115

HOW TO MITER A CORNER ON THE BACK

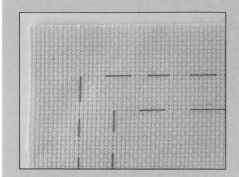

1 Baste along the fold line around the edges of your work, then baste another line the depth of your desired hem inside the first line. Trim your fabric to the depth of your hem plus ⅜ in for turnings.

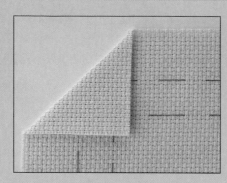

2 Fold the corner of the fabric to the wrong side at an angle of exactly 45° so that the fold just touches the corner of the outer line of basting. Press firmly with a steam iron to give a crisp line.

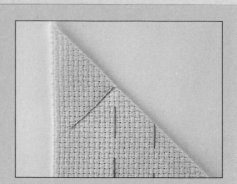

3 Unfold the corner, then fold the fabric in half diagonally, right sides together, so the two parts of the pressed line match. Stitch by hand or machine along the pressed line, from the fold to within ⅜ in of the raw edges.

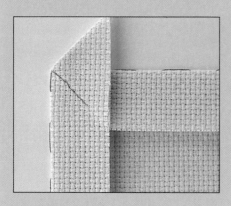

4 Open out the mitered corner and press the fabric firmly along the outer basted line, so that the hem lies flat on the right side of the fabric.

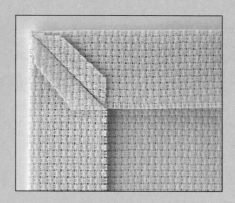

5 Trim the mitered seam and clip the corners to remove the excess fabric. Press the seam open so that it lies flat. Remove the outer line of basting stitches.

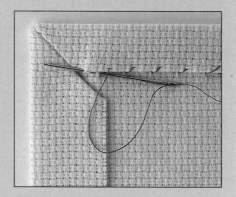

6 Turn the hem to the wrong side and press. Turn under the extra allowance so that the hem lies folded along the second basted line. Press, remove basting, and stitch down hem.

HOW TO MITER A CORNER ON THE FRONT

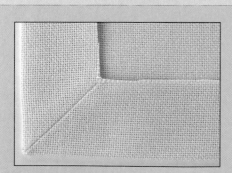

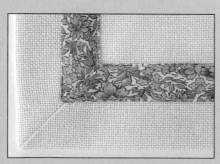

The easiest method is to stitch the miter in the usual way, but work with the wrong sides of the work together and stitch the seam right out to the raw edges of the folded line.

For a decorative effect, stitch a strip of binding or ribbon to cover the raw edges. Miter the binding or ribbon by stitching diagonal seams on the wrong sides at the corners.

WHAT WENT WRONG?

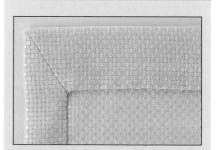

Here, the original fold for the miter was not made at exactly 45°. As a result, the miter is crooked; although it lies neatly, the unequal angles make the hem allowances uneven.

Making pillow forms

One of the secrets of successful pillow-making is having the right pillow form. Here we show how to make your own.

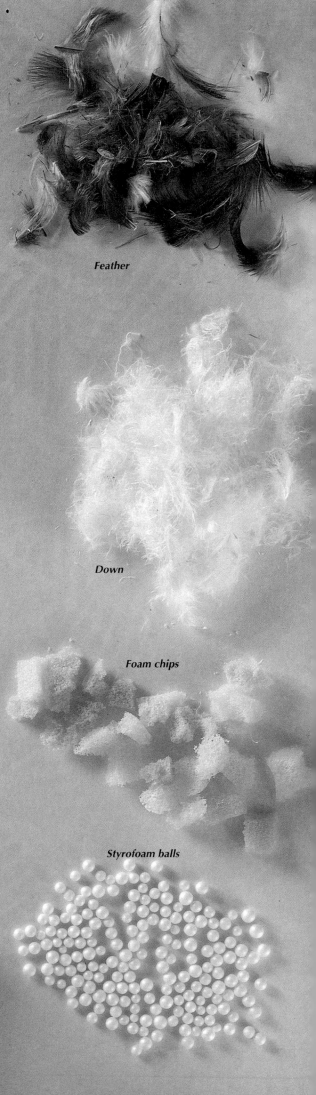

Feather

Down

Foam chips

Styrofoam balls

I f you want a pad for an unusual shape or size of pillow or just want to economize, it is useful to know how to make your own. Making pillow forms is straightforward; the steps are logical and can easily be adapted for different shapes and sizes.

FABRICS FOR PILLOW FORMS

The best fabrics to use are firmly woven cottons. They are easy to work with, keep their shape well without distorting under the pressure of the stuffing, and are cheap and readily available. It is best to choose white or cream, in case your pillow cover is thin and the pad shows through, though if you are making pads especially for dark pillow covers, you can use leftovers of dark cotton fabric.

Firmly woven cambric, cotton sheeting, or similar fabrics are very good and usually cheap. Chintz and polished cotton can be used, but are more expensive. Many people use muslin, which is cheap. The sizing that is used on some cotton fabrics, including muslin, as well as the firm weave, help the fabric – and therefore the pillow form – to keep its shape. If you are using feathers or down as a stuffing, it is worth paying more for down-proof cotton. If you don't, the feathers may work their way through the fabric.

STUFFINGS FOR PILLOW FORMS

Many materials are available as filling for pillow forms. Your choice will probably depend on the size and type of the pillow, the desired texture of the finished pillow and how much money you want to spend.

The most expensive stuffing is **feather**, or a mixture of feathers and down. Down is the extra-fluffy feather-like material that grows under a bird's main feathers. Feathers and down give a smooth, satisfactory finish with just the right amount of squash or give.

Foam chips are cheap and readily available. They tend to give a more springy feel to the pillow and can be quite hard if the pillow is firmly stuffed. The smaller the chips, the better the result, but avoid very cheap versions that are full of big, firm lumps. Also, make sure that any foam you use is flame-retardant.

Styrofoam balls are ideal for large floor pillows or items for which you need a filling that moves around to take on the required shape rather than one which is just springy. These, too, are very cheap, but care must be taken as they can give off noxious fumes if they catch fire. Also, they do eventually compress, so you will have to top up your floor pillow after a while.

Other stuffings include **kapok**, a natural stuffing which is soft but which can tend to flatten or go into lumps, and **synthetic filling**, which has the benefit of also being washable.

When making your own pillow forms, it is very important to bear in mind the safety aspect of the materials you plan to use. Whenever possible, choose flame-retardant fabrics and fillings.

Kapok

Synthetic filling

HOW TO MAKE A SQUARE PILLOW FORM

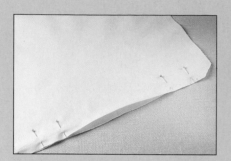  

1 Cut two squares of fabric the size you want your finished pillow form to be plus seam allowances. Stitch along the seam line, leaving several inches open in one side.

2 Clip the corners, turn right side out, and press. Fill with stuffing through the gap; don't over-stuff, or the pillow will be too firm.

3 Fold under the raw edges around the gap; pin them together, then machine-stitch neatly close to the outside of the fabric to close the opening.

HOW TO MAKE A CIRCULAR PILLOW FORM WITH A GUSSET

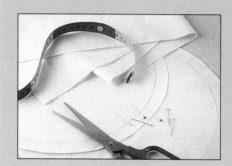  

1 Cut two circles the size of your pad plus seam allowances. Measure the circumference. Cut a gusset to this length by the required depth, plus seam allowances.

2 To make the gusset, stitch the ends of the fabric strip to form a circle, then pin, baste, and stitch around one circle, right sides together, easing the fabric around the curve.

3 Attach the gusset to the other circle in the same way, leaving a gap for stuffing. Trim the seams, then turn, fill, and close by hand or machine-stitching.

bright idea

For a scented or herbal pillow, put some potpourri or fragrant dried herbs inside the pillow form. Mix them with some stuffing as well; otherwise, the pillow will be hard and lumpy.

WHAT WENT WRONG?

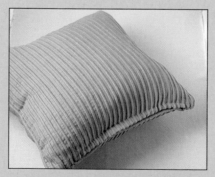 

It is important to put in just the right amount of stuffing. The aqua pillow has been filled with a form that is too big and too firmly stuffed; the shape is distorted, and the pillow has no squash or give. The plaid pillow has a pad that is too small and flat; it has lost all its shape and cannot provide any support.

Applying piping

Piping in a matching or contrasting fabric sets off all manner of pillows and upholstery to perfection. Here's how to achieve a professional finish.

To show any type of pillow off to look its very best, trim it with corded piping in a color and fabric of your choice. It is not at all difficult, and it gives a very neat, professional edge. A variety of effects can be achieved by using piping in a color complementary to the pillow, in a contrasting color, or one of a different texture.

MAKING PIPING

Although it is possible to buy ready-made piping in standard colors, or braid specially set on a strip which can be applied like piping, making your own is very easy to do.

When you are buying piping cord, you will first need to measure the edges of the pillow which you wish to trim and allow at least 4in for turning and fraying. If you intend to wash the finished pillow cover, it is a good idea to wash the piping cord itself before you apply it in case it shrinks.

Select a gauge of cord which will suit the weight of the fabric and size of the pillow. Now you can choose whether you want to use ready-made bias binding or cut bias strips in a fabric to match your pillow.

For bias binding simply buy the same length as the piping cord, in a width that will leave you at least a 1-inch seam allowance when it is doubled over the cord. Bias-cut fabric stretches perfectly around corners, so it is ideal for this kind of trimming, but if you want to make your own binding from a piece of material, you will need to cut your own bias strips of fabric.

CUTTING BINDING

First lay out your fabric as shown in the steps overleaf and fold the horizontal grain of one end up to lie along the vertical grain. Press the fabric along this fold with a warm iron and then cut along the fold. Now all you need to do is cut strips of the required width,

keeping parallel to this first cut. Cut a width which will leave 1 inch of double fabric free when doubled over the cord.

To trim a pillow, you will need to join several strips – do this following step 3 (over) to make a continuous strip. Press the turned seam so it lies flat, and trim the edges evenly.

To make the piping itself, fold the binding in half along its length, wrong sides together, enclosing the cord. Pin and baste firmly so that the stitching is right next to the piping cord.

APPLYING THE PIPING

Lay out the fabric for the pillow front, right side up, and mark a 1-inch seam allowance all around. Take the piping and, starting in the center of one side, pin the piping along the seam line, the cord lying just inside the seamline, carefully shaping it around the corners.

When you come to join the two ends of piping in the seam, cut the cord inside the two pieces to abut exactly and cut the binding

on one end even with the cord. Trim the binding on the other end to within 1¼ inches of the end of the piping and fold under a 1-inch hem. Pull this end over the other end of the piping to cover it like a sleeve; then, making sure it is lying flat, pin and baste it in place all around.

Stitch the piping in place, either by hand in backstitch, or by machine using a zipper or piping foot to keep the stitching close to the piping cord. Snip the corners of the binding so they lie flat at the corners. Place the back of the pillow over the front, right sides together. Pin and baste in place around three sides and stitch over the previous line of stitching.

Fill the pillow with a suitable pad, then fold back a 1-inch allowance down the edge of the backing, and fold in the piped edge along the line of the stitching. Pin the two together and baste in place, then slipstitch together to complete the pillow.

Choose a fabric to complement the color of the pillow for a really professional finish.

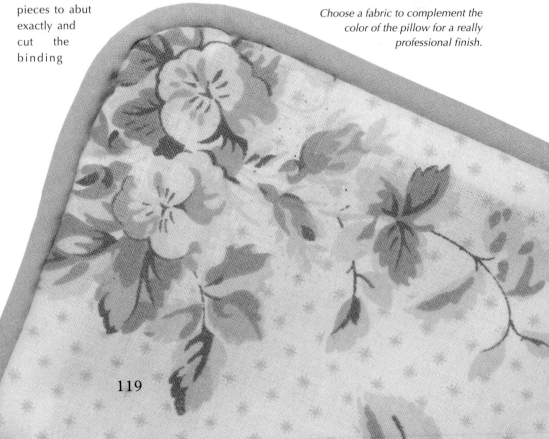

119

HOW TO MAKE PIPING

1 Mark the horizontal straight grain of the piping fabric and fold it up to meet the vertical grain. Press this diagonal fold to form a sharp crease, then cut along the fold to give one edge of the bias binding.

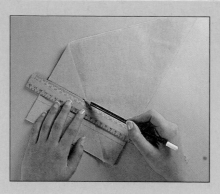

2 Depending on the thickness of your piping cord, mark lines an appropriate width from the diagonal you have cut, keeping them parallel. Cut strips to give the length of binding you need.

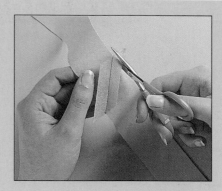

3 To join two strips of binding, place two ends right sides together so that they form a right angle. Make a 1 in seam, then press open so that the binding forms a continuous strip. Trim off the triangle edges.

4 Take the piping cord (washed if necessary to prevent shrinkage) and lay along the center of the wrong side of the binding. Fold to enclose piping cord, matching the edges, and pin and baste next to the cord.

5 Press the fabric for the pillow front and mark a 1in seamline all around it. Pin the piping to the right side of the fabric, matching the basted line to the seamline and curving the piping at the corners.

6 Where piping ends meet, cut the cord to abut and trim one end of binding even with its cord. Leave a 1¼in overlap of binding on the other end, press in a 1in hem, and pull it over the short end. Pin in place.

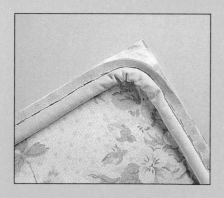

7 Stitch the piping to the pillow front either by hand using backstitch or by machine using a piping foot to keep the stitching close to the piping cord all the way around.

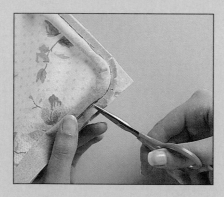

8 At the corners, snip the binding to within a couple of threads of the stitching so that it fans out and lies evenly against the pillow front. Press and mark a seam allowance on the pillow back.

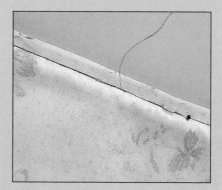

9 Attach the back to the front on three sides, right sides together, pinning along the stitching and keeping the cord inside the seam. Turn right side out, insert pad; turn in open edges and slipstitch.

Cords and braids

Making your own cords and braids is surprisingly easy, and they can be used to add the perfect finishing touch to all kinds of projects, from accessories and garments to pillow covers.

Cords and braids have many uses to the needleworker. You can make fine or textured versions and incorporate them into embroideries and needlepoint projects, or use thicker cords for couching down with stitches in a contrasting thread. Or you may find that you want an edging for a piece of embroidery, such as a throw pillow or footstool cover. For all these different uses, it is very satisfying to make just the kind of cord or braid you want, in exactly the right thickness, using the perfect colors of thread.

WHAT ARE CORDS AND BRAIDS?

Cords are simply twisted hanks of thread. The mistake that many people make when they are making their own cords is to try to use a single twist of thread. Stable cords, which do not unravel easily, are formed from double twists, where the batch of threads has been twisted tightly and then allowed to double back on itself. It is much easier to use a cord for your projects when it is not trying to unravel all the time.

Braids are plaits of threads. The traditional braid is made from three hanks of threads plaited together, and this is the easiest kind to make if you are a beginner, but if you are good at plaiting, you will know that more than three hanks can be plaited at the same time. The principle is just the same, but using more hanks takes a little practice and is best done on a flat surface such as a macramé board so that you can see where you are. If you use hanks of different colors, you will be able to see very easily whether you have kept the hanks in the right order as you plait.

MATERIALS TO USE

Both cords and braids can be made using the same thread throughout, or using a mixture of many different threads. You can make both cords and braids with any kind of thread, from the finest silk to the thickest yarn, but remember that some threads are so fine that you will need many lengths to make a braid or cord of a significant thickness.

If you want a very fine cord or braid, you will need to use a very fine thread to make it, or just use a few strands of a coarser thread. So, for instance, for a fine cord to edge a silk-covered box, you could twist quite a large number of strands of silk thread, which is very delicate and twists very tightly, or just a few strands of a thicker thread such as pearl cotton. If you want a thick cord, you could use many strands of fine thread such as floss, or just a few strands of a thick wool yarn. Remember, though, that if you are making a cord, the final cord will be twice the thickness that you see when you have made the preliminary twist, because you allow it to double back on itself.

Both cords and braids look very effective made in a selection of threads of different colors and textures. If you are making an edging for a particular project, try to use the leftover threads from the project itself, blending the colors so that they reflect the color mix in the piece of work. If you are making something for a subtle piece of work, blend the colors of your cord or braid subtlely; similarly, if you are making an edging for a bright, bold piece, be more adventurous with the color choice for your cords and braids.

The cords and braids shown here can be homemade, using threads varying from thick, matte cottons to fine metallics. These examples demonstrate well the different effects you can achieve by varying the colors, textures, and thicknesses of threads.

HOW TO MAKE A FINGER BRAID

1 *Wind a hank of thread twice the required length of the braid. Cut the looped edges at the bottom. Secure the top to a solid object, such as a chair back, or with a thumbtack.*

2 *Divide the large hank into three equal hanks of thread and begin plaiting them, taking the hank from each side in turn and weaving it over and under the others.*

3 *When you have plaited the whole length of the threads, secure the end with a knot so that the braid cannot unravel. The braid is now ready for you to use.*

HOW TO MAKE A FINGER CORD

1 *Cut lengths of thread three times the required length of the cord. Knot the ends. Tie or hook the top around something solid, or pin it securely to a wooden surface.*

2 *Using a pencil, keep the hank taut and twist the threads steadily in one direction until you have twisted the whole hank firmly. Bring the end of the hank up to the top.*

3 *If you have made the preliminary twist firm enough but not too tight, the two halves of the cord will twist smoothly and securely together and will not unravel.*

bright ideas

There are endless threads and yarns that can be used to create unusual cords and braids. In these two examples, knitting yarns have been used to create textured effects.

The upper example is a plaited finger braid which has been made from three fancy knitting yarns of the same weight.

In the lower example, a mohair knitting yarn and a smooth ribbon yarn have been combined to make a twisted finger cord. This has been loosely wound to make the most of the sheen on the ribbon yarn.

WHAT WENT WRONG?

Your cord will not work properly if it is twisted too tightly. In the example shown here, the cord has been over-wound so that it has become distorted and irregular instead of forming a neat, double twist.

Making tassels

Tassels look spectacular and can add just the right finishing touch to a piece of embroidery, they are surprisingly easy to make, and you can produce them in exactly the size and color scheme that you require.

All the tassels here are homemade and illustrate the variety of styles that can be achieved.

Handmade tassels are immensely satisfying to produce; they look spectacular, and you can make them in exactly the threads and colors that you require. Most tassels that you can buy are heavy ones suitable for items such as curtain tiebacks. When you make your own, you can produce smaller, lighter tassels that are just right for your own projects.

USES AND MATERIALS

Tassels are useful for providing visual interest in embroidery and needlepoint. They can be formed in the traditional way, by winding loops of thread, or you can use stitched tassels or a batch of knotted threads for a smaller, finer tassel. Larger tassels are ideal for the corners of projects such as embroidered pillows and can also be used on clothes, for instance, around the yoke of a jacket or coat. A glittery evening bag would look wonderful finished off with a few tassels made from the same glittery thread you have used to embroider it.

You can make tassels from virtually any thread, but some threads work better than others for some kinds of tassel. If you want to make a small, dainty tassel, use relatively fine threads such as stranded floss, pearl cotton, flower thread, even ordinary sewing or buttonhole thread. Remember that, as with making cords, the finer the thread, the more strands you will need to make a tassel of a particular thickness. Although you could make a small tassel quickly from just a few strands of thick yarn, the beauty of tassels comes from an even distribution of many threads, and a small one made from thick wool yarn would miss that attractive finish.

If you want to make a very large tassel, you could use thick yarn, but the disadvantage of wool is that it tends to become unwound very quickly so that the strands lose some of their definition. Even for a very large tassel, a mass of finer threads looks more spectacular; you can bulk out the finer threads by adding some strands of matte cotton.

There is no need to make a tassel entirely from one thread, or even all of one color, unless you want to. Mixtures of threads and colors add texture and visual interest to the tassel, and catch the light in different ways. If you are making tassels to finish off a needlecraft project, use your leftover threads for the tassels, mixing them in roughly the same proportions as they appear in the design. For example, if your embroidery features a few bright colors on black, make your tassels predominantly black with just a few bright-colored strands.

HOW TO MAKE A TASSEL

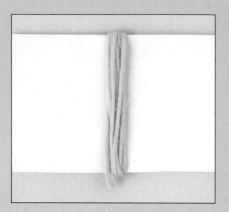

1 Cut a piece of cardboard the depth that you want your tassel to be, then wrap your thread around it – a few times for a fine tassel, many times for a thick one.

2 Use a bodkin or tapestry needle to slip a length of matching thread under the tops of the loops, and tie the thread tightly to catch the loops together.

3 Using small, sharp embroidery scissors, cut through the ends of the loops at the bottom of the cardboard.

4 Using another length of matching thread, wind it tightly around the loops near the top and fasten off to make the characteristic tassel shape.

5 Use a tapestry needle to take the ends of the tying thread down through the body of the tassel to hide them, then cut the ends of the tassel so that they are even.

STITCHED TASSELS

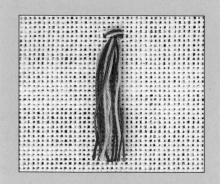

Thread a large-eyed needle with several lengths of thread. Take a small horizontal stitch from right to left, leaving a long end of thread. Make another stitch beside it, taking the thread ends through the loop. Pull tight and trim the ends to the required length.

A simpler way of stitching tassels is to take a small horizontal stitch through the fabric, leaving two long ends. Tie the ends in a single knot and then trim them to the required length.

bright idea

One of the most attractive methods of decorating the top of a tassel is with a covering of blanket stitch. Thread a tapestry needle with a contrasting thread, bring it up at the center top of the tassel, then make a series of blanket stitches into the central point. Keep the stitches free by looping them around themselves rather than stitching into the body of the tassel. Continue working around and down the tassel top, then work the final row of blanket stitches into the tying thread to prevent the decoration from slipping off.

Mounting cards

Making your own cards gives you the pleasure of presenting a lasting gift to loved ones. Pre-cut card blanks are available from craft stores in many shapes and sizes.

MAKING A GREETING CARD

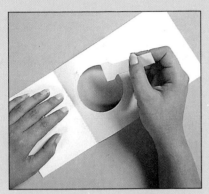

1 Trim the edge of the embroidery to fit inside the window, then spread fabric glue sparingly over inside of the central section of the card. Make sure that no glue gets onto the face of the card.

2 Lay the embroidery right side up on a flat surface and position the glued area of the card on it so that the stitched design fits the window. Turn the card over and smooth the edges of the fabric.

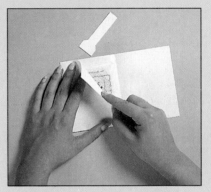

3 On the inside, spread glue sparingly around edges of center section, avoiding area where fabric shows through window. Fold left-hand section of card over to cover fabric. Press down firmly to seal.

Number chart

The numbers on this chart can be used on a variety of projects.

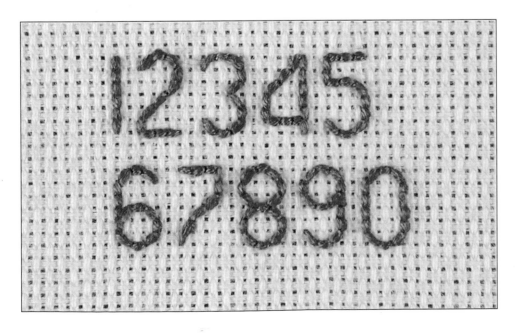

These charted numerals are used on the Celebration card on pages 53–4, worked in Holbein stitch and back-stitch. Adapt them for use on a sampler, or work them on other greeting cards or commemorative gifts where using a date would be appropriate.

Mail-order kits

As an added benefit to our readers, we are able to offer a selection of the projects in this book as mail-order kits (see list below). All kits include aida fabric, needle, Madeira 6-stranded embroidery floss, stitch chart and instructions.

For prices and availability, please contact:
Shillcraft Inc.
8899 Kelso Drive
Baltimore
MD 21221
Tel. (800) 566 3064

Should you not require any of the offers listed below, you may still like a FREE copy of Shillcraft's craft catalog. Send your name and address to Shillcraft at the address on the left and Shillcraft will rush a copy to you by return.

ITEM	CODE	DESCRIPTION	PAGE
1	72749	Cactus pillow kit	13
2	72201	Clematis pillow kit	17
3	72316	Gladioli pillow kit	21
4	78292	Rose sampler kit	25
5	72301	Bouquet picture kit	29
6	72517	Cottage picture kit	33
7	72429	Kittens picture kit	37
8	72439	Deer picture kit	41
9	78487	Harbor picture kit	45
10	78338	Bird bell-pull	77

Index